We Should
Be So Lucky

Also by Kathy Levine

It's Better to Laugh . . . Life, Good Luck, Bad Hair Days, and QVC

Published by POCKET BOOKS

Kathy Levine

with Jane Scovell

We Should Be So Lucky

Love, Sex, Food, and Fun
After Forty from the Diva of QVC

Illustrations by Amy Sarah Appleton

POCKET BOOKS
New York   London   Toronto   Sydney   Tokyo   Singapore

To all of my cherished friends.
You know who you are and you know I love you.
We should be so lucky to grow old and off
our rockers together.

———

 POCKET BOOKS, a division of Simon & Schuster Inc.
1230 Avenue of the Americas, New York, NY 10020

ISBN: 0-671-00848-X

First Pocket Books hardcover printing October 1997

10 9 8 7 6 5 4 3 2 1

Printed in the U.S.A.

Contents

Contents

Foreword

Hello Again! It's me, Kathy. You asked for it, and just as I promised, I'm back between the covers of a book. Assuming that you all know that it's better to laugh, this time I'm going to be talking about life after forty, okay, maybe after forty-five, but you get what I mean—I'm talking second half here, and it's my chosen task to tell you how to make the most of your silver and golden years!

My theory about life after forty is simple: "Try it,

buy it, diet, but do it." And, to illustrate my philosophy, I'm going to cover a variety of subjects from romance to health and beauty.

As far as romance, I don't know about you, but for me, dating the second time around is a major issue, especially since the ongoing search for the perfect date means you have to subject yourself to a never-ending parade of *im*perfect dates. I ought to know, I've gone out with them all: the short and the tall, the fat and the small, the poor and the poorer, the almost right and the totally wrong, the old and, here's the twist, the young(er)!

Once I get through with the men in my life, it's on to health and beauty. I'm going to let you know about my efforts to stay in shape. I'm going to talk about my *body*—you know my bra size went from 36B to 36 Long, my stomach went from a molehill to a mountain, and my thighs went from slim to thunder—and my *face*—yes, I confess, there's something to tell. And I'm going to tell the truth about the breakthrough diet program that changed *my* life. (Remember, I used to be the girl who never ate one of anything, except a turkey.)

I'm also going to tell you about the influence of the Internet on my life. Hey, when 350 e-mails say there's something wrong with your face and your figure, it's time to look in the mirror. I'll be talking,

Foreword
Foreword

too, about people I know who've been caught in and nearly strangled by the Web.

Before I've finished, I'm going to touch on something that all of us will come up against after we've passed the midway mark—mortality. Suddenly, it's not just "older" people who die, it's your contemporaries.

I lost my best friend, the most important person in my life, and was devastated to the point where I couldn't think straight. You know me, I'm the biggest cockeyed optimist in the world, still, I had to work hard, very hard to find the Kathy my family, friends, and viewers have come to know.

Anyway, I'm back now, and I've put down all my experiences. I'm sure you'll feel right at home reading about many of the situations I've run into and if you don't, trust me, it's just a matter of time. Oh, one more thing, I always try to use real names but here and there (you'll know where) I've had to change them to protect the guilty as well as the innocent.

Onward to life after forty. Enjoy it, be over the top, not over the hill, and don't regret anything.

x i

Introduction

by

Richard Simmons

Well, to tell you the truth I was so nervous the very first time I appeared on QVC. To start off with, it was the dead of winter. West Chester, PA, where QVC is located, looked like a ski resort, and yes, I was in my tank top and little candy-striped shorts.

It's quite an impressive building. You have to go through security and then you're led down all these hallways. A metal door opens and you're in the Willy Wonka of cable home shopping. The room is huge, with hundreds of operators taking calls. Computer screens just everywhere. And people buzzing around. Well, let's just say I was a little farklempt.

I made my way down the main aisle and all the operators started to wave at me and then there I was at the producer's desk watching the robotical cameras and listening to all the cues like a maestro conducting an orchestra.

All of a sudden I hear a voice, a very distinctive voice: "Honey, you'll have nothing to worry about. It'll be fun. They are just going to love you." I looked around, and there was this lady standing there with these beautiful Bambi eyes. There was not a stitch of makeup on her face, not a stitch! Maybe a little moisturizer. Her hair was in rollers . . . rollers, pink fuzzy Velcro rollers. And then I looked at her hands. They were Streisand-like, long smooth elegant fingers topped off with a freshly painted French manicure.

Yes, this was my first Encounter with the Queen Bee of QVC, the royalty, Kathy Levine. (Please pronounce her name correctly: It's Levine, like in *Vin*-cent Van Gogh. Don't pronounce it like "Heard It Through the Grape-*vine*." She gets very upset.) I'm so proud to say that for six years Kathy has been my friend. If you watched us together on a show, you know that is pure love. We do have the best time. We laugh so much it's truly like visiting her home and staying to sell a few items.

What do I like most about Kathy? She treats and greets everyone with care and humor. She always tries to brighten up someone's day. She is kind to people on and off the air. You will never know of the good she does for people because she never talks about it. She has touched many lives. She sure has touched mine. And just by reading this book your life will be touched, too.

Well, I could go on and on but Kathy has many books inside of her so I'll have to save a few stories. Enjoy the laughs.

1

Young at Heart, or, Lead Me into Temptation!

I'm not sure how long *lust* lasts, but as of this forty-five-year-old moment, I assure you it's alive and kicking.

Being a full-blooded female, *passion* remains near and dear to my heart—hey, I'll probably be dating in the Home for the Aged. "Temptation" is my middle name and when it comes to romance that old serpent doesn't have to push hard for me to take the bait. I've always been an equal opportunity

1

dater, I date anything with a pulse, but as I've grown older, the question of whom to date has arisen. In general, I've always toed the line when it came to the suitability of my suitors. For one thing, they had to be age appropriate—I dated men my age and older and never looked the other way until fate sent me into new dating territory.

I had a bone in my foot operated on in the spring of 1996 and for six weeks QVC was nice enough to cover the table I sat behind with a long cloth to cover the ugly boot I had to wear. For a month and a half, I worked and I sat, and I worked and I sat and when I wasn't sitting and working, I hobbled around. I couldn't exercise, I couldn't travel, shop, or entertain, and was soon beyond bored. I was restless and itchy for fun and that's when my first adventure began.

My friend Renee dropped by one evening and the two of us sat around brainstorming ideas about how to meet men.

"They say," Renee offered, "if you get a dog and walk it, you'll meet someone."

"Renee," I said, pointing to the black-haired schnauzer in my lap, "what would you call Chelsea, a stuffed panda?" Now, you all know my dog is the love of my life, but in seven years, she's never led me to anything but the nearest hydrant.

"Sports!" Renee cried out.

"Like what?"

"Like tennis. You get all outfitted, and you go and sign up on the courts and before you know it, you've got a partner."

"Forget it," I answered. "Men don't go out onto the courts looking for women. They usually come with a partner and, anyway, even if they are alone, they get caught up in the game."

The conversation continued in this manner—good-natured Renee coming up with a variety of options and cranky Kathy shooting them down one by one.

"Hey," I blurted out after dismissing a safari to Kenya as being a bit far-fetched, "what about an ad?"

"You've got to be kidding," said Renee, now the scoffer. "You mean we should answer one of those single personals?"

"No. I mean we should take control and place our own. Give our credentials and let them come and get us!"

This brilliant thunderbolt was followed by a quick trip to the local mall, where Renee and I picked up a bunch of magazines and newspapers featuring want ads for warm bodies. We took our pile and went through the listings, and this is what I learned—the operational word is *seeks*. Everyone is seeking. Divorced white female SEEKS; single

Afro-American businesswoman SEEKS; voluptuous model SEEKS; personable doctor SEEKS; sexy Latin lady SEEKS; college-educated widow SEEKS; sassy contortionist SEEKS, etc., etc. Talk about competition! So many women were seeking I felt my ship sinking but it was Renee, in fact, who dropped out.

"Kathy, I wish you all the luck in the world, but I can't do this. I'm going to a singles ski happy hour next week. You're welcome to come along but I'm not putting any ads in any papers."

And so, my partner-in-the-crime-of-trying-to-find-Mr.-Right and I came to a parting of the ways on this issue. She followed her path and I plowed into mine. I consider myself a pretty with-it type, someone who'll take a chance here and there, especially when it comes to broadening my social horizons. I have a few friends who've had real success with personal ads, and while I don't think they're the be-all and end-all, they do provide the opportunity to meet people. They perform a function that matchmakers once fulfilled, only you're much more on your own with personal ads; you have to be your own matchmaker. It's very important to pick the right place to put your ads, I mean in respectable magazines and newspapers, not underground stuff.

Determined to create, in print, the world's most magnificent mating cry, I went over those personal ads with a fine-tooth comb, figuring I would learn from other people's efforts. Sure enough, a pattern emerged. No matter what the wording, the ads boiled down to a simple "loving, warm, compassionate person looking for a relationship." Some of the embellishments on this basic theme really made me laugh. How about this statement: "Loves fine dining." Is this an incentive? Who likes bad dining? And how about ads that read "Loves long walks in the park"? Hey, let's face it, I do not need to take a long walk in the park. I want to be with somebody who's going to be fun and has some energy and takes me places that I like to go. The truth is, if a guy called up and said, "Let's go for a walk in the park," most women would say he was cheap. I could go on and on, but I'll cut to the chase.

I selected a newspaper that I thought was a good respectable venue for me, a tristate publication with an ample concentration of executive-type readers. In other words, this newspaper was fairly upscale, so I wouldn't be putting myself out in some wacko arena. I'm really amazed at the number of people who don't do a thorough check before they put their life story on the line. Do that and I think you're bound to wind up with weirdos.

I called the paper and discovered that their system was quite simple. First, you put in a written ad, which runs for two weeks. Once it was placed, you were connected to a voice-mail box and allowed to leave a three-minute message telling more about yourself. This way, anyone who was interested could hear your voice and your style. As far as the written ad, since you paid per word, it seemed to me that a short message would tip off any prospective suitor that you were "stingy." You know me, my ad was about the length of the Gettysburg Address and cost me a whopping $160! Plus (and I must add this), I was told that for an extra five dollars, the entire blurb would be put into bold print, thus making it stand out from all the rest. Another cute idea and worth the fiver.

I made up my mind that in composing my text, I would avoid the traps I'd seen—none of the general hearts-and-flowers B.S. for me. I decided to laser in and be really taut and arrogant. By echoing Popeye's "I yam what I yam," I figured someone would read through and see a witty lady who was different from the rest and who definitely rated a call. In pursuit of my honesty's the best policy approach, I had to avoid standard bugaboos, e.g., age. Personal ads invariably read, "I'm forty-five but look thirty," or "youthful fifty, looks forty" all that kind of stuff. The problem is because people drop years from their CV, the person who answers gets a mental picture that doesn't jibe with the actual person and the first meeting can be scary. You go expecting to see Demi Moore and you're face-to-face with Grandma Moses. I think I'm pretty youthful looking but I wouldn't set myself up for that kind of fall. Okay, enough exposition, here's my masterpiece as it appeared in its final **bold** form:

> **Successful businesswoman, 44, but looks 43. I work like a lunatic, travel too much, and get one Saturday in a Blue Moon off. Forget the cuddling and long walks in the park, I have my dog for that. I would like to enjoy an occasional dinner or play in Philadelphia or New York with a very bright creative man who makes me laugh. You must be proud of who you are and your accomplishments. Age, older or younger, not important, but a beautiful smile and meticulous grooming are musts. Big boozers and smokers need not respond.**

Wouldn't you think a piece of work like that would bring in replies galore? I sure thought so and eagerly awaited the deluge.

Before I actually placed the advertisement I called my mother on the phone and read it to her. After I finished, a long pause ensued.

"Kathy, dear," she said softly, "don't you know that you get more flies with honey than vinegar?

You're never going to get anybody with that ad. You sound bitchy."

"I am bitchy," I snapped back. "I'm just being honest."

Usually I listen to my mother, but this time I was hell-bent on my own course of action.

Into the fray went my ad. Oh, I should say it went in among all the other **bold** type copy. Everyone chose to spend the extra five dollars; consequently, nothing stood out.

Next, I recorded the voice message, even more to the point than my written notice: "Hi. You have reached box number 12345. My ad reads" . . . and then I reread the thing. When I finished I said,

So, enough about you, let's talk about me. I'm five-seven, pretty, in a Barbra Streisand, Donna Karan way—without the nose.

I have a very difficult schedule and appreciate someone who is flexible beyond Saturday night only. I love theater. Off-off Broadway is great and I attend theater in Philadelphia whenever possible. I howl over Larson's Far Side and will miss Erma Bombeck. I enjoy Jake's in Manayunk, Cobblefish, and Judy's Café for get-down-and-dirty dining and I'm game for most any food except sushi. In New York I have a hundred little treasures which I'm only too happy to share with you.

My dream experience would be to sit in Oprah's chair for a day or to sit in on a brainstorming session for a hot new product at an advertising agency. I love exchanging ideas on sales and marketing. As for you, I would enjoy positive high energy and clear direction. Also, someone who is well read and well bred. Good manners are never optional.

By the way, I have no preference about hair except if you have one strand that you coil around your head like a yarmulke, I will die.

Leave your name and number if you wish and we might be chatting soon. Thanks for calling.

I telephoned my mother and read her what I recorded.

"You're a dead duck, dear," she sighed. "No one is going to want to talk to you."

I thought she was 100 percent wrong. I mean, by reading it my personality emerged, my sense of humor, my interest in sales and marketing, and the fact that I was a Streisand lookalike and that I liked to eat. I wasn't trying to pass myself off as a blond, blue-eyed Vanna White. I'm not a kewpie doll, I'm an ethnic. I really thought that along with being cynical and off the wall by mentioning Erma Bombeck and Larson, anyone could hear that I had a left-sided sense of humor. I sincerely believed that I was describing myself pretty accurately and that I would attract a certain type.

According to the system, after you entered your message in the voice-mail box, you could check for "mail" once a week . . . for free. If, however, you were antsy and couldn't wait, you could phone the mailbox as many times as you wanted and pay one dollar per call for the privilege.

Even though I was dying to know if anyone was answering, I still managed to contain myself for five whole days before I broke down. No way could Curious Kathy hang around for seven days waiting; it was like hanging around to hear about a pregnancy test. I made my first call on the sixth day and from then on averaged four calls per day. By the end of the month I had a $120 phone bill.

My first call netted a positive result! I had one message. I was so excited that this was it, I was pressing the dress for my wedding and placing the invitations in the envelope.

"Hi," said my future husband, "my name is Bob. I'm five feet six so I really don't know why I'm answering your call since you're five feet seven. But, what the heck, what's an inch or two between friends? Do you ever give up control? You obviously like to be in charge. Maybe somebody else should be in charge for a change. You're very bright, you're very successful, you're extremely funny, and you're probably somebody I'd like to meet. So, if you want to call, here's my number."

I put down the receiver, counted to three, okay, two and a half, and called him back.

Of course, I got an answering machine. Now, according to the rules of the game, I couldn't leave my telephone number because that would have left me exposed. I was warned that I should not give information about where I lived or anything like that because Jack the Ripper could be looking for a date. You had to make personal contact first and then assess the situation. Bob wasn't there, so I simply left a message on his machine saying, "Hello, this is the voice-mail that you answered, successful businesswoman forty-four looks forty-three. Obviously, I'm not allowed to leave my number. I'll try to connect with you at another time."

For a while, our machines were doing the connecting and, with hindsight, frankly, I think the answering machines should have dated.

At last, Bob, in person, picked up the phone. First off, he wanted to know what I did, and since I didn't want to say I was a show host, I told him I sold jewelry. At the risk of repeating myself, I shy away from identifying my profession because television implies celebrity and money and I don't want that. Anyway, when I said I sold jewelry, he said, "Oh." I could "feel" his expectations drop. I was sure he was envisioning me as a girl behind the counter in a department store hawking costume jewelry. Immediately I upped the ante by saying that I worked for a worldwide distributor of gold and silver.

"We do a lot of business," I confided, "and I travel a lot. I have a very busy schedule, which is why I ran the ad. I don't have much opportunity to meet people, that is, eligible people." That stated, I turned the tables.

"What do you do?" I asked.

"Well," answered Bob, "it's sort of complicated."

"Hey, I've got a sixth-grade education, give me a shot," was my reply. Oh, mouth of mouths, I was doing it again. I had to be a wiseass.

Bob told me he was a technical engineer in a very specialized field. Thanks to my all-around knowledge accumulated in selling everything from soup to nuts, I immediately knew what he did and was even able to ask him if his company was like a well-known organization with a similar product.

"Oh," said Bob, "you really do know what I do."

"Hey, I told you I had a sixth-grade education."

Bob chose to overlook my snappy comeback and moved on to another area. Actually, Bob and I were beginning to resemble oil and water before the shaking. I was definitely floating on the top and he was drowning, or vice versa.

"Now tell me more about yourself," he said.

"Well, as the ad read, I'm five feet seven but I give a big appearance."

"What does that mean?"

"I mean I wear heels. I'm a big girl. I have a big persona. I walk into a room and am perceived as five feet ten."

"You sound like a giant," groaned Bob. "I mean what the hell are you wasting my time for?"

"Excuse me," I replied, "you answered my ad and I wrote five feet seven. If you're five feet six, that's your problem. Do you have a problem with that?"

"Well, I'm only saying that you make yourself sound like a dinosaur."

"And, I'm just trying to tell you that I wear heels and give off a big presence." What I really wanted to say was that I had fingernails taller than he was, but I was controlling myself.

"I just would like to ask you one question," said Bob. Once more into the breach and I answered, "Yes."

"Do you," he inquired, "have children?"

Okay, now we're on solid ground, he's probably worried about dating someone who's got a brood of kids, and I quickly answered, "No, I don't."

"Well," he replied, "we have a problem. May I tell you why?"

"Sure," I said.

"It's my experience that women who've never had children, and I know this because I've had long-term relationships with women without children, don't understand unconditional giving. You don't know what it's like to sit up all night with a feverish child or how to be there for a child who's had a traumatic day."

"Oh." Now it was my turn for "ohing."

At this point, the dress was being returned to the bridal store, the invitations were being canceled, and we weren't going to make it to the first date—this man had smoked me beyond smoke. I was pissed.

"Let me ask you something, Bob, these relationships with women without children, how long did they last?"

"Oh, a long time, three or four months."

"An eternity, Bob, an eternity." My blood was boiling. Three or four months and this joker is an authority. How dare this man, this Bob, talk to me that way? How did he know that I didn't lose a child? How would he know if I didn't at some point have a miscarriage or something? How does he know about the unconditional giving I may or may not have given? Has he had a husband who had cancer? Did he have to put his father into a nursing home? How dare he say that!

I spoke calmly and slowly. "You know what, Bob? I would never want to disagree with you. You have a point of view and I'm thinking, okay, let's just call it a day."

"I agree. Good luck to you."

"And good luck to you."

I hung up the phone. Once the receiver was nestled in its cradle, I let out a scream and proceeded to pace like a wildcat. Why did I open myself up to that kind of verbal abuse? How dare this person tell me what I am or am not based on having a child? So everyone who has children is the most wonderful unconditionally giving person in the world and someone who hasn't had a child is a brick? Give me a break. I was fried. I called my mother, I called my friends and regaled them with the story of this miserable mumzer who value-judged women on the fruit of their womb! I wanted my money back. I wanted my ad stopped. I wanted to forget the whole damn thing.

For a while, anyway.

The next day, I called into the voice mail and found another message waiting. Hope springs eternal. Get the dress out, get the invitations out. I listened to the caller and two seconds into his communication, I knew this wasn't one to answer.

16

"Hi, my name is Richard. I'm eighteen, but your ad said younger didn't matter. I like older women and I hope you'll answer me because this call is costing me a fortune!"

I hate to admit I didn't even return his call and if you're out there somewhere, Richard, I apologize. I owed him the courtesy of an answer but I could tell right off the bat this kid was looking for someone to take care of him . . . a sugar mama, and that was not my intention.

My ad ran for two weeks, and you have up to a month to get responses. About a week after Little Richard phoned, and just as the ad was running its course, another caller left his message in a deep, delicious-sounding voice: "Hi, my name is Dave. I'm a big fan of Larson's *Far Side* and as far as my fantasy, I don't care about being on Oprah, I prefer walking along the beach with a big golden retriever at my side and an ice cream cone in my hand."

Immediately my ears perked up. This was someone who read what I wrote and was using what I said to his advantage.

"I'm a 'recovering doctor,'" continued Dave, "that is, I went all the way through medical school and then decided that I hated the sight of blood. I'm finishing law school next fall."

I nearly dropped the phone. A doctor *and* a lawyer! This was a Jewish woman's dream! I pressed

17

the phone to my ear so hard it nearly came out the other side of my head.

"People tell me I look like Jeremy Irons. I'm five feet nine, an excellent tennis player, and no, I do not sport the single hair curled around my head like a yarmulke, so don't worry. If you'd like to call me, let me know. Oh, I'm twenty-nine but my friends tell me I look thirty."

Despite the sudden shock at his youth, I didn't even count to one, I clicked off and on the phone and dialed Dave's number. He was there in person and the first thing I said was, "Why is a twenty-nine-year-old man answering an ad from a forty-four-year-old woman?"

"I have had two thousand blind dates in the past few years," answered Dave, "because my mother and all her yenta friends set me up over and over again and none of them has held any interest for me. My mother was totally exasperated and one day she was reading the paper and saw your ad. She came over to where I was sitting and threw the paper down on my lap.

"'Okay, Mr. Big Shot, since no one is good enough for you, how about trying this lady on for size!'"

Can you believe it? Dave's mother was playing Cupid. Of course she did it out of sheer aggravation and never anticipated the result, but it's a lesson for all you mothers out there—don't push your sons

18

too far. By the end of our conversation I decided that if Dave was willing to go out with an old fart, I was willing to go out with a young sport.

Our first meeting took place on June 10 and Dave turned out to be a darling! We met at a trendy Philadelphia restaurant—so trendy it was on the second floor. I climbed the stairs anticipating that my young date would be there in a stroller with a box of Pampers in hand. Not!

I have to say, the minute I saw him, I liked what I saw. He was good-looking, trim, and, true to his word, five feet nine and with a full head of hair. He was funny and witty and, most important, an attentive listener. While we talked he looked me straight in the eye, and boy, do I like good eye contact. I can't stand that shifty business where you get the feeling that the person you're talking to is involved with someone over your shoulder.

Okay, he's young, I thought, but he doesn't look that young and I didn't feel old next to him. Even though I wouldn't say it in my ad, I think I look five years younger. And Dave looked five years older. We balanced out at thirty-five—at least that's what I told myself to feel better about robbing the cradle. I had told Dave that I sold jewelry. Remember? I try to stay away from my television persona; I like to be judged for myself, not by my screen career. Dave didn't have a clue as to my profession; he's not a television watcher and had no idea that I was a TV personality. We were halfway through the meal when a man came barreling over to our table waving paper and pen in his hands and crying, "Kathy Levine! Kathy Levine! My mother loves you. Sign this." I signed while Dave watched, saucer-eyed. After the gentleman left with his autograph, Dave said softly, "Is there something you'd like to tell me?"

On our second date I had tickets to the theater, and true to my written word, I wanted someone to escort me. Along with my coworker Bob Bowersox and his wife, and Judy Crowell and her date, I had purchased tickets to one of the hottest shows in Philadelphia, *Love! Valour! Compassion!* and I asked Dave to join us. Okay, this was our first official date and we met outside the theater and proceeded inside where we took our seats—center orchestra about six rows back.

I introduced Dave and I could tell that my old friends thought he was an okay guy. You just know when someone blends in. The curtain went up, the play began, and within eight minutes most of the actors had dropped their shorts and were standing in the altogether. I had no idea male nudity was part of the show and my eyes opened *wide* when the exhibition began. My God, I thought, I could have taken him to a Chippendale show. I leaned over and whispered to Dave.

"I'm so sorry, I didn't know it was this kind of play. I hope you're not embarrassed."

"Oh, no," he answered, "I'm not embarrassed in the least. I'm fine."

Well, I was glad that *he* was fine because I was dying. All these guys tripping and bouncing around the stage and I'm on a first night out with a kid. I held my breath for a while and then I figured, oh, for Pete's sake, he's seen it before and so have I and what am I supposed to do? I relaxed and thoroughly enjoyed the play, it was quite wonderful.

Sitting next to Dave in the theater, I knew that we had some chemistry going. I could feel something as my arm brushed against his on the side of the chair. Some things never change no matter how old you are. I was trying to negotiate my elbow, you know, trying to figure out where I could put my arm to let him know that it was okay for us to be brushing against each other. A couple of times I'm sure he started to take my hand in his but didn't quite make the move. It was so silly and so fourth grade . . . and so much fun. I'm not sure how the others viewed our antics, I only know that there was an electricity between me and this young man.

After the show the Bowersoxes and Judy and her date departed. Dave and I decided to go for a drink.

He took me to the Ritz Carlton Hotel. (The kid had taste.) We talked and talked until three-thirty in the morning, when security finally threw us out. Then we sat in my car and talked until dawn.

"Dave," I said as we sat there sleepy-eyed, "I want to ask you something."

"What's that?"

"My ad said that I was interested in dining and going to the theater and things like that, but I'd like to know what you want."

"Whatever *you* want," he replied.

"Oh no you don't," I said. "You can't slide like that. Let's put it another way. Are you looking for a romantic relationship or are you looking for someone to escort occasionally?"

"Whatever you want," he said yet again.

"Okay, let's put it another way. Let me ask this a little more clearly. Would you like to kiss me or do you just want to take me to the theater?"

"I'd like to kiss you," he answered with no hesitation.

I was ecstatic. Call the printer, get the dress.

Dave and I started dating, and kissing, and then some, and were doing fun things from the get-go, "things" that I might not have classified as "fun" for me before I started going out with him.

"I'm an outdoor kind of guy," he told me. "I like fresh air." He was the athletic type and an excellent tennis player and before you could say Steffi Graff, I was in and out of the store and outfitted in a little white pleated uniform. Who makes those dorky outfits anyway? Dave took me out to the courts and reintroduced me to a game I always loved but rarely played. He was such a pro. He stood in one spot while I raced around like a wild banshee, chasing from side to side, screaming, cursing, throwing my racket to the ground, and clutching my chest for air. It was 90 degrees and the humidity clung to me like a cheap shirt. He was twenty-nine and I was forty-four, I was dying! I so thoroughly enjoyed myself with the Fresh Air Kid. Our tastes meshed and our humor was identical. We laughed our tails off. I'm always impressed by brains, high moral character, and humor—the formula for unbelievable chemistry, and we had a very clear chemistry.

Flushed with my success on the courts, Dave encouraged me to try running. Here's my take on that activity: If you're forty-four you shouldn't run. Gravity wins every time. Everything fell in the first ten minutes. My chin was on my boobs, my boobs were on my knees, and my knees were on my ankles. One quick jaunt and I hung up my "running" shoes for good.

Jogging was out but everything else stayed in as Dave and I continued to enjoy each other's company. We went for walks in the park, we went to the zoo, we went to the theater, we went to New York and dined at fancy restaurants, and then we'd go down to Chesapeake, Maryland, for crabs. We were all over the place and we each tried to cater to the other's likes and dislikes. I happily back-pedaled my own rather sophisticated palate and ended up eating fish sticks rather than trout amandine and Dave upscaled his preferences to accommodate mine. One night we were in a sidewalk hot dog stand and the next we were in New York City's chichi Trattoria del Arte. I introduced Dave to gourmet dining. B.K. (Before Kathy) he ate one dish and one dish only, chicken parmesan. If it wasn't on the menu, he'd leave and go somewhere else. I have nothing against chicken parmesan, but I noticed that he was locked into it. One night we were at an Italian restaurant in King of Prussia and after the waitress left the menus, I asked him what he was going to order.

"Chicken parmesan," he replied.

"Come on, Dave, you always get the same thing. Try something different."

"What if I don't like it?" He pouted.

"If you don't like it, I'll take your dish and you can eat mine."

"What are you going to order?" he asked.

"Chicken parmesan."

Reassured by my choice, Dave screwed his courage to the sticking place and ordered risotto. I wish you could have seen the expression on his face when the waitress brought the risotto to the table. His nose turned up, his lips curled; he was sure he was going to hate it. He took a bite, and then another, and, of course, he loved it! Now he had the whole world in his hands, he could order *two* dishes!

When it came to fine dining, Dave didn't get the importance of wine and was just as happy to order a bottle of Thunderbird or a bottle of beer. Well, that's okay for cheeseburgers but when you're dealing with real cuisine it's so nice to accompany the food with the appropriate grape. Before I educated him, Dave was of the "all wine tastes alike" school. One evening, to prove my point, I bought five bottles of five different vintages and brought them home. I opened the bottles, lined them up, and Dave and I proceeded to do our own tasting. At the end, Dave learned that all wines are not alike; he learned the special vocabulary for describing the bouquet and taste of wines. No, we did not drink all five bottles, nowhere near it, just enough to taste.

It wasn't just on the subjects of food and drink that Dave and I got together, it was everything. We went to concerts and while my choices were relatively mainstream, he introduced me to music I never heard before. I took him to hear Celine Dion one night and a few weeks later, he took me to hear

Sarah McLachlan, one of the newer singers. And that's how it went.

I never felt like I was old with him. I was dressing younger and managed to cram myself into a pair of jeans that were so tight I had to stand at the movies. I started wearing jeans and T-shirts and blazers and cute sneakers (size 10 cute). I even put

GAGA!

on a little bitty mini top and there was my pupik hanging out between the bottom of the top and the top of the jeans. Dave didn't care. He thought I was darling. He thought I was the best thing since milk chocolate and he never mentioned age. He always complimented me, always told me I was sexy and that I had beautiful eyes and gorgeous legs. He saw all the good things that I, like so many of us women, chose not to see. I'm always complaining that my rear end is too wide for my middle. He didn't see that, he thought I looked fabulous. He saw me as an attractive woman. And what did I see? I saw a healthy, lean, dynamic man I loved looking at. I showed him off like a Judith Leiber handbag. He was a treasure and I couldn't believe this treasure wanted to be with me. Not that I'm bad, but he was a young man with a whole world of resources out there and he chose to be with me!

We were a terrific-looking couple (if I do say so myself!). We went to parties and he provided a breath of fresh air in some of my tired social life. My friends started calling me Mrs. Robinson. Before they met him, they called Dave the "pup." They'd telephone and say things like, "Hey Mrs. Robinson, we're having a party on Tuesday. Why don't you and the pup come by." But, when we did show up and they met him, they liked him and he became one of the gang. Listen, he wasn't four, he was twenty-nine and he fit right in.

Okay. I know you're dying to ask—"Why did I date a twenty-nine-year-old?" It's a fair question. Look, so many of my male peers had gotten heavy and sluggish and depressed. I've dated my fair share of contemporaries and, quite frankly, the grass seemed so much greener in the younger fellow's yard. I like my men to be physically fit, and the truth is, a lot of guys my age let themselves go. I take pains, and I do mean pains, to keep myself in shape, and I expect the same of my partners. When I'm introduced to someone, more than his scintillating personality, I want someone who has a zest for life and who's in shape, and the older you get, the more important that becomes. You can have all the money in the world, but if you've got a coronary, what's the difference?

Believe me, there's plenty to be said for younger men. They're game to try most anything, they don't have a lot of emotional baggage, and they don't mind telling you up front what's bugging them. Many times we'd get together and Dave would say right off the bat, "I'm having a problem today. Here's something you said and it's been bothering me and I want to talk to you about it." Then, he'd repeat what I'd said and we'd talk about it and all the time I'm thinking isn't this different from being with those "turtles," those older guys whom I ordinarily date, who just pull in their heads and hide in their shells. You have to rap on the cases and make with the "Hello, is there something wrong?" And, they say, "No, no, I just don't want to talk about it," and then they go and bury themselves in front of the television. Dave wasn't like that. He challenged me and that's what I wanted. It didn't matter that I was older; he didn't care that I was famous on QVC; if he was angry with me, he told me so. He took no garbage from me and I loved the refreshing "in your face" approach of someone who wasn't afraid and wanted to try things and do things.

And you know what? A part of me wanted to feel the way a man feels when he wakes up in the morning and has this young beautiful trophy next to him. Why just men, why not me? If it's good for the gander why shouldn't it be good for the goose?

As much fun as I had, I didn't go into the relationship with my eyes shut. I mean, fifteen years is a big gap. Let's face it, though, if the positions were reversed and *he* was a decade and a half *my* senior, no one would have blinked an eye. A guy shows up at a party with a three-year-old and everyone says, "Oh what a lovely girl, where would you like to sit?" They give him a drink and her a

Shirley Temple, and all's well. I'm exaggerating but I see this kind of stuff all the time. Everyone expects that when a fiftyish man divorces or is widowed, he's going to come around with a P.Y.T. (Pretty Young Thing) who's in her twenties or thirties. Everyone expects and accepts that, but when a woman chooses to go out with someone who's young, healthy, and vibrant, she's a dirty old lady and must be footing the bill. It's not fair and it's not true. People are people. Age is irrelevant . . . sometimes.

I walked in with my eyes wide open and so did he. I knew at some point Dave had to move on in his life. He was starting a career and I was too old for him. There's a bittersweet quality to a lopsided romance. Mind you, even though I knew from the start that there was built-in heartbreak and anticipated the outcome at the onset, I don't think that it always has to be that way. Many women have married men who are sixteen and seventeen years younger, but you have to bear in mind that if a man clearly wants to have a family, you've got a problem. Having been married to someone who desperately wanted children, I knew firsthand that no man should be denied that joy and privilege. Dave loved kids and was very clear about wanting children of his own. It was obvious to both of us that we were together just for a while and that was okay, I accepted the terms and my, oh, my, what a run we had! When I was with him I was young, I was sexy, I was desirable, and I was lively.

People who saw me on television that summer said I looked fabulous. "You're glowing! What is it?" asked my viewers. "It" was like I had been sent to Fresh Air Camp for the summer—I looked fresher. My advice to anyone in a similar situation is, go for it. Don't worry about what anyone says, do what your heart tells you to do.

Of course, my mother, the parole officer, had her doubts from the beginning and from day one kept reminding me of the temporary nature of my new relationship.

"Honey, you know this young man is going to want to move on," she admonished and, being a card-carrying Jewish mother, added, "Just think about how *his* mother feels. She must be plutzing that her son has chosen someone closer to her age."

Actually, I did meet his mother and his father, in fact I met his whole family. They were warm and delightful and his mother and I could easily have become friends, we were on the same wavelength. She was very smart. She left her son alone to make his own assessments and in the end, common sense on both our parts prevailed. She didn't need to nag or bug him. . . . She just let time pass and the reality check set in. Dave and I spoke honestly about the future and how it would take him five years to set up a successful practice. We talked about the children issue and actually had a brief hallucination that my tired old ovaries would crank up for one last hurrah. I saw myself lumbering onto the set of QVC with this huge belly, support hose to keep my varicose veins from spilling out, granny glasses slipping off my nose, and a glass of prune juice in my hand. Oy. It just wasn't going to happen. Furthermore, I began to realize that while we complemented each other's tastes, the financial differences were another story. I always had to be sensitive to the money issue. A fun night of theater and dinner could easily set someone back $150 and this guy wasn't even working yet. Whereas it was easy for me, it was a stretch for him. Playing pool was great, having a sandwich and going to a movie were fine, but ultimately the little differences can begin to eat away at the good in a relationship and you find yourself picking at each other. Long before that could happen to Dave and me, we had a heart-to-heart and decided to turn the romance into a friendship. We made an agreement to try to do all the things we enjoyed doing just as before, but to do them as friends. The first few times were awful. We'd meet somewhere and he'd look at me with those big brown puppy eyes and we'd sigh and moan and lust after each other. In time, though, it got better. Fortunately, my attention was somewhat diverted. About the same time I met Dave, I was asked out on a blind date by a doctor (my mother's dream come true). I explained to him that I had just started dating someone with whom I was rather smitten. It is not my policy to date more than one man at a time, so I couldn't see the point of having a drink or dinner with the doctor while I was dating Dave. Never one to let anything, or anyone, slide off the hook completely, I asked the doctor if I might re-call him at a later date if and when my current flame extinguished. I'm honest—blunt, too! He was disappointed but reacted graciously and agreed that I could call him in the future. Thus, when my relationship with Dave took its turn into friendship, I had someone to call. This took the pressure off me, and Dave. I began seeing the doctor. Meanwhile, Dave and I accomplished the near im-possible—we became friends. We can hang out together, laugh, go to a movie, take a walk, visit each other's home, and as my original ad requested, he is still a favorite escort. I know that someday I will dance at his wedding and I will embrace the woman who chooses to be his life partner because she'll have to be one special as well as one lucky lady. Dave's going to be a wonderful husband and for sure he'll be a better mate as a result of our time together. At least he won't always be taking his wife out for chicken parmesan, and he does know a red from a white wine.

All told, Dave was no mistake. I got my $165 back tenfold and although I will not place another ad, I'm sure glad I did it once. I had the best summer of my life and, equally important, my time with that marvelous young man gave me a lift that's still in effect. He pulled me out of the tired, comfortable, and comforting ambiance with which I surrounded myself and into a whole new world. I did something that perked me up and I didn't worry about whether or not it looked "nice" to others. At my age, looking nice doesn't count anymore, feeling nice is what matters.

2

The Meet and Eat Club, or, Please Pass the Pepto-Bismol

During a recent long, not-so-hot summer, my girl-friends, the yentas, and I got together to solve the problems of the world. Did we discuss global warming? Health care? The economy? No! We were talking about men, and naturally we were addressing that really important issue—the best way to meet someone. A few yentas wanted to try the personal ad route, but, having "been there, done that" I was searching for a new path.

Once you've reached a certain age, and boy, I've reached it, a lot of natural resources—school, clubs, the workplace, singles bars (ech)—get pretty much exhausted, but the "fix-up" remains a good bet. Granted, there have been times when I've been fixed up and the only thing my date and I had in common was the fact that he was male and I was female. This, I assure you, goes only so far. Most of the time, though, my friends and relatives try to match me with someone who's compatible. It's so much easier when another party makes a formal introduction for you; that way you get the history or background up front. For sure the fix-up is a good deal but unfortunately, it doesn't always happen.

How many times have you said to friends, "If you know anyone let me know," and they answer, "Okay but I've got to get rid of my cousin Sally first, or my husband's sister or . . . etc. With all the pitfalls, I do think that being matched up by friends is about the best way to go. My advice is, if you get a chance to take a blind date, snatch it. If it doesn't turn out, well, the worst thing you've lost is a night of watching QVC!

So there I was sitting with the yentas, including my old pal Renee (whose happy hour for skiers had yielded zilch), trying to think of clever ways to meet eligible men, and by eligible I mean not married.

The problem is, a lot of guys who *are* married cling to the strange notion that they are still eligible. You wouldn't believe the number of attached men who are ready and willing, even though they are unable, to date. I bump into these guys over and over again when I'm on the road and I've learned how to handle them. You've got to weed those putzes out and in order to do that, you've got to have what amounts to a dossier on any potential escort or, at the very least, a brief Q and A session with the interested party. You want to get the lay of the land, if you get my drift. Even so, I count on friends like Renee to delve into the nitty-gritty of dating. Renee is more scientific than I. As you know, I tend to fall into situations whereas Renee does her homework, and on this particular night she told me about the fruits of her latest labor.

"Kathy, I saw an advertisement in the paper and I think it'll work for us."

The word *advertisement* has a special resonance for me. Remember this is the girl who got her job at QVC through an ad that a friend saw in the paper. Right away I was all ears and I told Renee to continue.

"I was looking in the personals," she said, "and I came across a dating service that sounds good."

I bristled at the words *dating* and *service* being

We Should Be So Lucky

linked together. I've seen advertisements for dating services on television and they looked pretty hairy to me, definitely not my cup of tea.

"Hey, I want to go out," I said, "but I don't want to be with some paid gigolo."

"No, you've got it wrong," explained Renee. "This isn't an escort service, it's a gourmet dining club for singles called Meet and Eat. They run a series of dinners at local gourmet restaurants for unattached men and women."

Again, I was troubled. Gourmet restaurants—in my neck of the woods? I mean, there are a few lovely places to dine but for the most part, this is a meat and potatoes, or maybe a fish and chips, area. Oh well, when it comes to food and men, I'll always give the okeydokey to any situation that promises one or both, so I bit.

"What the heck, why not!"

Renee fished a bit of newspaper out of her purse and handed it over to me.

"Look, the next meeting is at a Mexican restaurant and we still have time to sign up."

I looked at the ad and I have to admit, it seemed pretty legit; the last paragraph read something like: "Get together with people you'll enjoy meeting. Our next intimate dining experience is Monday, April 22, at Mi Casa es Su Casa. Make your reservations now and rest assured that our policy ensures that

38

reservations are *equally divided* between men and women."

I had to admit, even though I never thought of Mexican food, above the border anyway, as a gourmet cuisine, and I'd never heard of the restaurant, the deal sounded pretty good. Forget the gourmet part, the ratio of men to women appealed to me. I checked my calendar and saw that I was free that evening.

"Let's go for it," I told Renee, and before you could say *Caramba!* we had reservations for dinner. Two hot tamales were on their way to finding a couple of chimichangas. Ole! Or should I say, Oy Vay.

On the appointed night, I picked up Renee. She was wearing a short, red "ooh, ooh, look at me" skirt and matching knit top; I was wearing what fit—a navy pantsuit. (I'll get into gluttony later, but you have to know that I was fat again.)

We drove to a mall in the next county and, sure enough, a gleaming red-and-green neon sign flashed the name of our destination. Oh, and behind the flashing Mi Casa es Su Casa, a huge cactus, on top of which hung a large sombrero, was outlined in glowing lights. Somehow this particular presentation did not add up to "haute cuisine" in my mind, but there was no turning back.

Monday nights are usually slow in restaurants.

People are broke or hung over from weekend partying, and consequently, it's a pretty smart idea to turn your place over to a specialty group, and that's just what Mi Casa es Su Casa had done. I parked the car and with a few quick makeup adjustments on both our parts, Renee and I got out and walked into the restaurant.

The minute the door closed behind me, I had a sinking feeling in my gut. Sure, I wanted to meet a man, but I respect my stomach, too, and a certain aroma hovering in the air, the same stagnant scent that greets you in any number of greasy roadside taco joints, gave me pause to reflect that maybe, just maybe, we were light-years, not a few steps, away from gourmet dining.

I looked at Renee and she looked at me and for a brief second, flight seemed the natural course. Before we made a move, however, we looked over at the bar and saw lots of people crowded around laughing and talking and so utterly convivial our doubts faded. Hey, they were having a good time and by God, so would we.

Renee and I headed right for the bar, where we each ordered a margarita. By this time, I was getting kind of excited that the evening might indeed be fun. We were at the bar for ten minutes or so, and then were ushered into a back room, where the "intimate" experience would take place. A long banquet table had been set up for twenty-six diners. I did some quick calculating. Okay, twenty-six divided by two is thirteen, so there would be thirteen men and thirteen women. I wasn't bothered—I'm not superstitious.

As it turned out, even if I *were* superstitious, it wouldn't have bothered me since the number thirteen never entered into the intimate picture.

In the rush of arriving and getting into the arena, I never had the opportunity to do a head count and it wasn't until we were seated that I took a good look around and what I saw was female, female, female, female, female, male, female, female, female, male, female, female, female, male, female, female, female, female, male, female, female, female, male, female, female, female, male.

I'm not good at math, but you didn't have to be Einstein to figure out that the "equal ratio" was six to one in favor of the girls, or rather, the boys. Six to one! These were racetrack not dating odds, especially in view of the promise that an equal number of reservations would prevail. I grabbed one of the organizers, a female, of course, and put it to her.

"Isn't it supposed to be an equal number of men to women?" I asked.

"Well, ordinarily, yes," she answered with a

broad smile, "and usually it is evenly divided. I don't know why but tonight we seem to have gotten a lot of women."

"Seem to?" I questioned. "I don't see any 'seem to.' I see twenty-two women and four men."

The coordinator giggled. "Yes, I guess you're right."

The nerve of this broad! I mean, the way she managed figures I could have used her as an accountant not a matchmaker. There was nothing to do but sit down and eat and reflect once more that, no matter how you slice it, it's a man's world. No matter where they were seated, those four guys were sitting in the catbird's seat. They could go down the line and be vile to eighteen of us and still have four remaining. It was like shooting fish in a barrel. They had their choice of twenty-two women and we women had to fight over for them.

The seating was prearranged and the coordinators did their best to place the scant few amongst the horde, opting to put three of the chosen ones in the middle of the long table and one poor chap way out in the suburbs. I guess the party planners figured they should pack the center and let the ends fall off so that conversation would go inward rather than be diffused. For some reason, I was seated in the central male cluster, between two of the men and across from the other one. Why had I

lucked out? I didn't have a clue. Anyway, at this point, I had stopped trying to figure out the modus operandi of the Meet and Eat Club, choosing instead to take a peek at our special prix fixe menu.

The menu was a destroyer.

Here's what it read: Frozen Margaritas; Scallops and Shrimp in Tequila Vinaigrette; Free-Range Chicken with Tex-Mex Tequila Barbecue Glaze; Intermezzo of Tequila Lime Sorbet; and Chocolate Mousse Tequila Pie.

I am not overly fond of tequila, at best, and this bill of fare didn't give me any leeway, everything was awash in the potent stuff. I wasn't sure from which end the explosion would occur but as sure as I sat there surrounded by veinte-dos señoritas and quatro caballeros, I knew there would be an explosion.

Looking around at my fellow diners, I guessed the participants' age range at thirty to sixty, something like that, except for the gentleman seated on my left, a widower named Mort who had to be in his late sixties or early seventies. On my right was a theology professor named Fred and across from me was a putz named Bernie. (Way down at the end of the table sat the gentleman whom I never met.) I call this Bernie a putz because from the minute the corn chips were placed in front of him to the moment the chocolate mousse was removed, the guy never lifted his head; the waitress put down the nacho basket and that was it. Obviously Bernie was far more interested in the "Eat" part of the Meet and Eat Club.

We participants introduced ourselves and went through the usual formalities: Where do you live? What do you do? Is this your first time? Most of the women were repeaters and had been involved in this and other singles clubs for years. No big surprise, the women were great and the majority were quite accomplished in their fields, heads and directors of companies. I said that I was in sales for a cable company and since no one knew me, or didn't say anything if they did, my story flew. On my right, Professor Fred announced, and I do mean announced—he didn't so much converse as lecture—that he was studying Eastern religions and had traveled extensively in China. As his lecture continued uninterrupted, I turned my attention to the carte du jour and pointed out an unknown edible to my fellow gastronomes.

"Look at this," I said, holding up the menu and pointing to a dish entitled Huachinanga (watch-ee-nan-ga), a word I'd never seen before, and don't forget, I speak Spanish. I decided to do a little shtick.

"You know, I think I had a case of Huachinanga once," I told the assemblage, "but three days of antibiotics cleared it up." Renee knows my sense of humor and started laughing and some of the other women caught on immediately that I was kidding around and joined in. One lady who worked for a pharmaceutical company asked which antibiotic I took, and another woman from human resources asked if I had to take a sick day. The head of a telcom company wanted to know if I used MCI or Sprint to report it. The women played along; the men didn't. Bernie ate, Mort sighed, and the

We Should Be So Lucky

learned professor went deeper and deeper into the Orient.

Professor Fred had deposited us at the base of the Great Wall when he suddenly interrupted his monologue, turned to me, and said, "Aren't we supposed to eat at seven-thirty?" I looked at my watch; it read seven twenty-five.

"What's your hurry?" I replied. "Got a late date?"

I wish I could describe adequately the stare I got. The guy hated me. That was the end of Fred the professor and I never looked right again. One down, three to go, although as I mentioned, I never even found out the name of the man off in Siberia.

I turned my attention to the putz across the table and at this point, Bernie was attacking the chip basket like it was Little Big Horn and he was Sitting Bull.

"Hungry?" I asked.

"Umm," he answered, raising his head for a split second, long enough for me to notice that he was suntanned.

"You've got color," I said. "Have you been away?"

"Yeh," the head snapped up again. "I've been to a Club Med. I love Club Med. Man, you can really meet lots of hot broads there. Great lays."

I assure you, he was not talking potato chips. Down went Bernie's head and off went the buzzer in my brain—the alarm that tells me I'm not where I would have been too crowded if all eight of us went in the back, I volunteered to sit with the driver. While the others piled into the rear, I slipped into the front. A book was on the seat and I moved it over to the driver's side, figuring he'd know what to do with it. The book was thick and heavy and the word *Law* stood out in the long title. The driver got in and immediately apologized for the book's being in my way. He spoke in a pleasant lilting brogue. I liked the way he sounded and I liked the way he looked. He was about six feet two with sandy blond hair and bright blue eyes, my type. (Well, one of my many types.)

"My name's Kathy Levine," I said, putting out my right hand.

"How do you do, Ms. Levine, my name's Ryan O'Sullivan," he answered as he shook my outstretched hand. He had a broad, friendly smile and a nice air about him. I was sorry the ride was going to be so short. Luckily, the fates intervened; we got stuck in a mondo New York traffic jam and it took forever to get to Lincoln Center. During this time the people in the backseat were caught up in their own conversations, so Ryan O'Sullivan and I chatted. I learned that he was from Ireland (actually, I figured that out myself) and had been in America for years. Ryan was about to finish New York University Law School, where he was second in his class.

want to be and not talking to whom I want to be talking. I resisted the urge to cry out, "Now, tell us, Don Pardo, what are the parting gifts for our losing contestant Bernie?" and simply avoided looking at him for the rest of the meal.

I had successfully eliminated two out of the three men in my vicinity. And then there was one, Mort. Mort was dear and sweet and using this opportunity, he told me, to come back to the world of the living. Mort's wife had been ill for a long, long time and finally, mercifully, had died.

Look, I'm a sympathetic person but I don't think that the lengthy and painful demise of a spouse is particularly scintillating conversation for a singles gourmet dinner. Mort obviously was in such pain, however, I couldn't cut him off. And so, from the scallops and shrimp in tequila vinaigrette through the tequila-glazed free-range chicken, I heard, in excruciating detail, the story of the onset of the disease and the eventual death of Mrs. Mort. The disease itself was never mentioned by name, and, forgive me, I couldn't help wondering if the poor soul had Huachinanga. Every night, Mort solemnly related, he would drag himself out of bed to change her catheter, and such were his narrative powers, by the time we got to the intermezzo of tequila lime sorbet, I could have changed that catheter myself. Trust me, during the course of that meal, I was thoroughly educated in the art of sustaining life for the terminally ill.

I was so depressed, I was so upset, I wanted to throw myself into the salsa. I needed sanctuary and with a signal for Renee to join me, I excused myself and went to the ladies' room.

"As God is my witness," I told Renee, "I will never do this again! I am going to kill myself, but first, I am going to kill the coordinator."

So what did I come away with from that evening with the Meet and Eat gang? Essentially, four phone numbers from four women I really wanted to see again. I repeat, the women were fabulous—sharp, funny, and witty. They came in all shapes and sizes and we ended up banding together—twenty-two women laughing our tails off, having a blast. Sometime during the evening, the men disappeared. We never even saw them leave. We gals just continued partying. It was a funny experience, all right, but datewise, neither Renee nor I netted any results, and, let's be honest, results were what we were after. So, I went headfirst into another avenue, one that turned out to be another dead end.

3

There's One Born Every Minute Starring Ms. Kathy Levine

Along with a group of seven coworkers, I was se up to an awards ceremony at Lincoln Center in N York City. Tova Borgnine, a frequent QVC presen and a lovely lady and friend, was involved with t ceremony and graciously arranged for a limousi to pick us up at Penn Station. We took the train the city, disembarked, and went out onto Eigh Avenue, where we found the car waiting at the cui The limo was big but not that big and realizing

Hey, NYU Law is a great school; Ryan had to be smart as well as cute. Now was the time to check him out. I glanced over at his hands on the wheel and noticed that he had a gold wedding-band-type ring on his right hand.

"Is your wife a lawyer, too?" I asked. Nothing like being blunt.

"Oh," he laughed, taking his hand off the wheel for a second and holding out his fingers. "I guess you think that's a wedding band."

"Well, it's plain and it's gold and I know that Europeans sometimes wear their wedding rings on the right hand."

"No, no." He laughed again. "This is a family ring. I'm definitely not married. I'm divorced."

"Oh," said Kathy.

The plot had now thickened; the attractive man next to me was unattached.

Ryan told me he'd been married for five years, divorced for three, and had a six-year old daughter named Tara. He broke into a huge grin when he mentioned his little girl.

"She's really something. The love of my life," he said proudly, "so darling and so beautiful. She's got long curly blond hair and the sweetest way. Matter of fact she does some modeling. She's in a TV commercial right now." Ryan described the advertisement and I remembered having seen it. A whole bunch of adorable children were in a plug for a health care plan or something like that and in the last scene the camera closed in on a little blond girl sitting in a swing. That beautiful child, Ryan informed me, was his daughter. I was very impressed.

"That's a popular commercial and it runs often. I hope she was well paid for it."

"Oh yes," Ryan said, "she got ten thousand dollars, but it's all put away for her college fund. She's in a Montessori school now and I'm paying for that with the money I get for driving." He turned to look at me for a second, turned back, thought for a minute, and then spoke again.

"Everything is for my daughter. I want her to have the very best. I go to school during the day and I drive at night. I'll be graduating in three weeks and I have to take the bar exams but I've already secured a position with a New York office. So my life's shaping up nicely, which makes it so much easier because I have custody of my daughter. That's kind of unusual."

I agreed. Unless she's a combination of Cruella De Vil and the Countess Dracula, a mother usually gets the kids in divorce cases.

"My ex-wife lives in New Jersey. She works in an Atlantic City casino," continued Ryan, "and when we got the divorce, I sued for custody. I didn't want Tara bouncing back and forth between New York and Atlantic City. Three days here, four days there, it's no way. I thought it would be too disruptive and I was able to convince the judge of that. Anyway, my ex-wife was just as relieved. That's one of the reasons we split, she didn't want the responsibility of a child. It worked out fine, though. I have a regular housekeeper and I try to limit my driving to evenings when Tara's in bed and full-time in the summer when she stays with my parents in Ireland."

"Do you have a picture of her?" I asked.

"Oh, sure, plenty of them, except not on me. She's really something, long blond curls, as cute as a button."

I really liked this guy. Forget his looks and brains, I'm a sucker for a man who's good to his kid, and Ryan glowed when he talked about his daughter. I got the warm fuzzies just hearing his story. And I must admit it didn't hurt that he was handsome, smart, and educated.

We arrived at Lincoln Center and got out of the limousine. Ryan said he would be waiting for us at the same spot at the end of the evening to drive us to our final destinations. The others had hotel reservations but I had arranged to stay at a friend's apartment. I wanted to do a little shopping the next day and see a few friends. I'm always game for a day off in New York.

The awards were fun, they always are, and when the show finished our QVC octet trooped out onto the Plaza and found Ryan waiting. This time I just popped into the front seat without any explanation.

Ryan dropped the others off and then it was just the two of us. We continued to chat till we reached my destination. He got out and came around to open the door. I stepped onto the sidewalk and, once again, put out my hand. I wanted to say how much I'd enjoyed our short time together and how I hoped we'd meet again. Actually, I wanted to ask him out sometime, but I just couldn't bring myself to spit the words out. I might be assertive in business but I still believe in boy meets girl and boy asks girl out. We looked at each other and there was a "pregnant pause." I had to make a quick decision whether or not to cross the line as a client, and he had to decide whether to cross the line as an employee. I think we both were aware of this but he simply reached out and took my hand.

"It was a pleasure meeting you, Kathy. I hope to drive for you again."

"My pleasure," I said, shaking his hand. I turned to go up the steps of the brownstone. He waited until I had opened the door and I turned to wave good night. He looked handsome standing there in the moonlight.

The next morning, at a respectable hour, I called Tova.

"Tell me about Ryan O'Sullivan," I asked after a few preliminary statements—actually one. "Hello, how are you?" I believe in getting to the point.

"He's a terrific driver," she answered. "I always ask for him when I come to New York. He's reliable, well-mannered, and prompt. And he's studying law." Tova didn't seem to know about Ryan's ex-wife and daughter so I let that go. Obviously Ryan was discreet and didn't go blabbing about himself to everyone. His revelations had come out of our heart-to-heart.

"Tova, I liked him a lot. I'd like to meet him again," I said forthrightly.

Tova caught my drift. "I'll call the service he drives for and get his number. I'll call you right back." She hung up and within minutes telephoned me and read off Ryan's number. "Just give him a ring."

"I can't just call him up, I'm too shy. I know it's silly but I'm not in the habit of calling men. What if he doesn't want to hear from me?"

"I'll call him." Good old Tova. True to her word she telephoned Ryan, told him the story, and got back to me.

"He was delighted. He'd love to go out with you. He didn't ask you because he felt it wasn't his place. I gave him your number and he'll be calling."

BINGO!

I put down the phone and within minutes it rang again.

"Kathy, this is Ryan." He spoke loudly and there was a lot of noise in the background. I said hello and told him I was having trouble hearing him. "I'm on a cellular phone," he explained, "and I'm standing in a laundromat." Ryan's washing machine had just died, he told me, and he had to take the sheets out to get cleaned.

"Where's the housekeeper?" I asked.

"Oh, she's off for the weekend." We talked a bit and then I told him that I was coming into New York in a couple of weeks and wondered if he'd like to meet for a drink.

"I'd love to," he said enthusiastically, "but you know I'm a poor college boy. I've got a lot of expenses. . . ."

"Hey," I interrupted, "I don't expect you to do anything special. I'm not looking for a big night out. I really admire what you're doing with your life and I like you, I just thought it would be fun to get together."

"It sure would be. I wasn't trying to back off, I'd love to see you, too. I just want to make it clear that I can't spend a lot of money. Whatever I have goes to my Tara, she comes first. But I'd sure like to spend time with you."

Ryan told me that he was taking his daughter over to Ireland that week and then coming back. How nice that he was flying her over—how expensive, too. I wondered how he could swing it, so I asked him. He explained that his father was a pilot for Aer Lingus and pilots' families got to fly for free. A nice break for a nice guy. We made plans to meet the week after Ryan returned and I wished him a bon voyage.

When Ryan returned, I invited him to join me at a friend's party in New York. We had a lovely time and all went well. I saw him again a few weeks later when I was in the city, and, once again, we had a great time together.

A short time later, an unbelievable hot spell moved in and toasted everything and everybody from Philly to Boston. Never mind frying an egg on the pavement, you could have cooked an eighteen-pound turkey. It was brutal, hot, hot, hot. I was supposed to go to New York to meet Ryan but I got to thinking: Here was this poor shnook sweating in the Big Apple while I lived in suburbia and had access to my girlfriend's swimming pool. Why don't I give him a break and see if he wants to come down here? I called his number, got an answering machine, and left a message for him to phone me. He called back later that day, again on that noisy cellular phone.

"Sorry for the static, I'm on Madison Avenue waiting for a client." We talked a bit and then I said, "Ryan, I don't mind coming up there but since my friends are away and I have a key to their home *and* their swimming pool, I thought you might want to come down here. We can have a swim and I'll get a bottle of wine and some munchies and we'll hang out till it's time for dinner."

Ryan loved the idea and was very appreciative of my "thoughtfulness."

A couple of hot days later, I picked him up at the Thirtieth Street Station in Philadelphia at 1:30 in the afternoon and we drove to my friend's place outside the city. I already had put a bottle of champagne to chill in the fridge along with a couple of pounds of big beautiful cooked shrimp. We reached our destination and while Ryan got into his bathing suit, I arranged a tray of the shrimp and cocktail sauce. I even found a bucket for the champagne. We went out on the terrace and the first thing Ryan did was open the champagne. We toasted each other and he immediately poured himself another glass. He offered me a refill but I waved him off, I hadn't finished what I had. The next thing he did was down the shrimp. He tore into those suckers like he hadn't eaten in weeks. Now, Ryan was very skinny, I mean not like a skeleton or anything, but really, really lean. Obviously he didn't eat enough and was making up for lost time. I was sorry I hadn't bought a cooked whale.

For the rest of the afternoon we sat in the sun, read newspapers, took refreshing dips in the pool, and talked and laughed. We had a terrific time but later it did strike me that I had, at the most, three shrimp to eat and one glass of champagne, which meant Ryan had the rest. By the time we got ready to leave at around 5:30, I was really hungry and looking forward to dinner.

I haven't mentioned her yet but you have to know that Chelsea was with us. Unless I say specifically that my pooch is not with me, ninety-nine times out of a hundred, she is. That afternoon, Chelsea did her usual dog stuff while we did our human stuff and my pup seemed to have had a good few hours for herself.

It was time to go, and Ryan, Chelsea, and I went to the car and what happened next I still haven't quite figured out. All I know is, Ryan opened the door and Chelsea jumped in. She went soaring by him, he shut the door and came around to let me in the driver's seat. A real gentleman. The front door, however, was locked, in fact, all the doors were locked, and what's worse, I had left the key in the ignition. During her swan dive entrance into the backseat, Chelsea somehow had hit the lock button and now she and the keys were sealed in the car . . . and the temperature hovered around 100 degrees.

I looked at my pooch and realized that there was maybe a twenty-minute window of opportunity before she would succumb to the heat. I panicked. Telling Ryan to stay with her, I ran into the house and called the Cadillac dealer. They told me it would be two or three hours until they could get out and give me a duplicate key. I grabbed the yellow pages and found a locksmith in the area. I called. He was gone for the day. I ran out to the car and joined Ryan at the window. Chelsea lay on the seat, her tongue was out, and you could see her poor little body heaving as she gasped for air.

"You've got to break the window," I said to Ryan. He nodded his head.

"You're right, I'll look in the garage for something to use." He came back with a golf club, a 5 iron I think.

"I'll break the side window," he said. "It's small and won't cost as much to repair as a big one."

That said, Ryan proceeded to smash the glass out, and then carefully reached in his arm, flipped the lock, and opened the door. Chelsea tumbled out, and I do mean tumbled. That dog was nearly parboiled.

Ryan swept out the pieces of glass and brought the golf club back to the garage. He found a piece of cardboard paper, which he fitted into the broken window, and we got in and drove off. Even though it was mine, I felt like I was a bum driving a stolen car.

I liked the way Ryan acted, I thought he'd been very heroic, smashing the window, and also considerate, breaking the smaller one to save money. BIG mistake. Later, when I brought the car in and told my story to the mechanic, he said, "Next time you're going to save a life, break a big window, they're much easier to replace." Who knew that the little side numbers in the back are custom made? It cost me three hundred dollars for Ryan's heroism and thoughtfulness, but I didn't blame him, I just learned my lesson: as opposed to diamonds, with windows smaller doesn't always mean cheaper. Frankly, I didn't care. I was so shook up over Chelsea's ordeal, it took me two hours to calm down.

We drove back to my place to freshen up and change for dinner. I am not in the habit of bringing comparative strangers, especially men, into my house to shower, however, at the time, it seemed A-okay; I do, after all, have two bathrooms and I'd been with the guy for an afternoon. Hindsight? D-U-M-B. Anyway, nothing untoward happened, we both went about our business, and then got back into the car. I dropped Chelsea off with my neighbor and Ryan and I continued on our way.

"I made reservations in a lovely restaurant in Philadelphia," I told him.

"I hope it's not an expensive place. I don't want to keep harping on it but you've got to remember I'm just a poor student."

"Hey, I invited you here and I know it cost money to come on the train. I'm paying for dinner. Besides, I owe you for saving Chelsea."

We went to this cute little restaurant, one of my

favorites, very intimate, very quiet. We sat down and the waiter took our drink orders. I ordered a glass of white wine and Ryan ordered a rum and Coke. The waiter brought over the drinks and put down a jigger of rum and a tall glass of Coke. Ryan didn't even look at the Coke and proceeded to straight-arm the rum. "I'll have another," he told the waiter. Ryan had three more rums and Cokes and I was kind of taken aback.

Truthfully, I hadn't been thrilled with the two thirds of the champagne bottle he'd polished off during the afternoon but excused that because it was so hot. I wasn't any more thrilled with the rum and Coke action at dinner, particularly since there was very little Coke involved. Obviously, Ryan knew how to handle his liquor since he remained totally sober.

I don't like guys who drink too much, but I have to say the dinner conversation was so interesting I forgot, somewhat, about Ryan's drinking. But, there was one other thing, he smoked. Now, I don't go for smoking, but I also realized that Ryan was a European and they're not as fierce about not smoking as we are in America. The first time he pulled out a cigarette, I said something and he was very nice and put the cigarettes away. He would not smoke in front of me, he said, however, he wasn't going to give it up for me, either. Okay, I thought, I try to let people do their thing even though it's not for me. Long term, I wouldn't tolerate smoking, but hey, this wasn't long term (yet), this was a get-together.

Ryan talked a lot about his daughter and about how important education was for everyone and how much he was looking forward to his upcoming job. On September 1, he was going into the New York State Attorney's office as a public defender at a starting salary of $60,000, not as much as could be made in other law offices but he felt that money was less important than being on the good side.

"I want to clean up things, get some of the junk off the street, and make this a better and safer world for Tara—and people like you, too, Kathy."

What a nice man, I thought. I was impressed, very impressed.

The only thing that stood between Ryan and his new job was the bar exam, and he was taking that in a couple of weeks. Ryan didn't seem overly concerned about passing, either; he said he felt confident that he'd do well and the pressure was off somewhat because his job was lined up.

Ryan's train wasn't till midnight so we went next door to a place that had music and dancing. We sat down and Ryan proceeded to drink three more rums and (no) Cokes. Oy.

The waitress put down the glasses, and the Coke looked at the rum but at no time did it get its feet wet. So, I was looking at a guy with a broad base of champagne and some fifteen ounces of rum in his body and there wasn't a sign—not a slur of speech or anything like that.

At this point I started to think something might not be real good here. And yet, he was not affected in any way that I could see by his intake . . . and, he was such a nice guy. I just chalked it up to the difference between the drinking habits of Europeans and Americans and after I left him off at the train I drove away thinking that despite my misgivings about Ryan's drinking, I'd had a good time.

Over the next couple of weeks, Ryan and I communicated by telephone. He called me a few times, invariably from some remote location with the sound of a crowd in the background. He was always tired because he'd just come back from working and was about to go to sleep. He was driving at night and sleeping and studying during the day. The bar exam would be the next week and he still wasn't worried. Hey, if he wasn't worried, neither was I. The man was second in his class and knew his stuff.

The following week I had another event in New York City, an American Cancer Society fund-raiser, and knowing that Ryan would be finished with the bar, I asked him if he'd want to celebrate by escorting me. Again he was pleased to accept.

"Have you got a tux?" I asked. This was a black-tie affair and renting a tuxedo can set you back a hundred bucks or so.

"What do you think I work in, Kathy? I have lots of tuxedos."

"Great," I responded and then made plans with him.

The night of the benefit, I checked into a hotel. Ryan called from the lobby, told me he had "aced" the bar exam, and came up to the room to get me. The minute he walked in the door I noticed that his tuxedo had seen better days, like maybe in the early part of this century. Talk about threadbare— the knees were shiny, the elbows were shiny, the sleeves were too short, and the pants were too short. Obviously, this suit was something he had driven in and sat in for years.

I don't mean to sound petty. You have to understand that looking good is part of my persona, especially when I go to functions where I'm representing my company as well as myself. I take great pains to look my very best and I'm used to being with someone who is similarly presentable. I was disappointed in Ryan's appearance but it wasn't his fault that he didn't have a suitable outfit, so I just kept my mouth shut.

At the fund-raiser we were seated with a well-known national broadcaster and her husband and a fashion celebrity and her husband. Need I say that everyone at our table was dressed to the nines except for my date, who was dressed to maybe the twos. Okay, Kathy, get a grip. What's important? The important thing was that he still was intelligent, fun to be with, and a caring father, even though he drank a helluva lot. Throughout the evening, Ryan excused himself from the table whenever he wanted a cigarette and aside from that, and the many, many rums and Cokes, and his rather tattered appearance, most everything else was fine.

Ryan hadn't taken a driving assignment until midnight, and when the benefit was over he walked me to my hotel.

"Are you excited about your job on the first?" I asked as we strolled along Fifty-seventh Street.

"Oh, they've moved it to September sixteenth."

"Why?"

"There are some things I have to do before and they're not quite ready for me. There's a training period and they moved my starting date. Anyway, it's just as well because I have to fly over to Ireland

and pick up my daughter. We're going to have a big family get-together when I get to my parents' farm." He talked about his mother and father and sisters and brothers with obvious affection and warmth.

We reached the hotel and said good night—okay, we kissed good night, and on the Kathy Kiss Meter, Ryan scored a ten, which made up for his low score in the clothing department.

I have to say, I was really attracted to this man and looked forward to getting to know him better, much better.

On September fifteenth, I phoned to wish him luck on his new job and left my message on the answering machine. He called later.

"Thanks for the good wishes, Kathy, but I'm not starting until October first. They thought it would be better to start at the first of the month." We talked a bit and I thought he sounded kind of low.

"Is everything all right?" I asked.

"Well, I miss my daughter."

"Didn't you bring her back? I mean school's started."

"Well, I thought it would be better if she stayed with her grandparents for a while till I got on my feet."

"Isn't she going to have a problem changing schools from country to country?"

"Maybe, but the way things are, it's still better than her being here while I'm in limbo."

We talked more. He really did sound preoccupied and I decided to end the conversation. I told him I'd call him again.

"Listen," he said, "I'm having phone problems so it might be tough to reach me. I'll call you."

"Look," I said bluntly, "is everything all right, is anything the matter?"

I kept pressing him till he reluctantly admitted that something was wrong—he was having financial problems. He'd lent money to a friend and now that person was unable to pay him back. "I know he's good for it but that money was in my savings account. I have a trust fund over in Ireland but I don't want to touch it because there's interest involved and transferring funds is expensive. Really, Kathy, I'm uncomfortable talking to you about this, so can we just skip it?"

"No," said Florence Nightingale, "you tell me what you need."

"Well, my rent is due, and I have some other bills due . . . and I'm short."

"How short?"

"Two thousand dollars. Eighteen hundred, actually, since I've scraped a couple of hundred together."

"How about my loaning you the rest?"

"I wouldn't take it. I don't want your money."

"Ryan, that's ridiculous."

Why was I doing this? I guess it's because I felt the guy was down and he needed a boost. I'm a sucker when it comes to situations like this, maybe because I feel that I'm so fortunate, I can be generous. Kathy to the rescue! I had a million reasons to justify giving Ryan money, starting with my admiration for his pluck at getting his law degree and his looking after his child. And didn't Tova know him for nearly a year? I simply thought he was a good guy in a jam.

I insisted on helping out, and eventually he accepted. He didn't grab at the offer right away, which made me feel that much more secure, and he hadn't asked for the full amount, either. A shnorrer would have gone for the whole entire sum. I told Ryan that I'd put a check in the mail.

"Kathy, as long as you're going to do it, would you make out a cashier's check and FedEx it to me? I didn't want to say it before but I need the money right away. My landlord isn't very understanding and if I don't pay him, I'm out."

"No problem," I said.

I went to my bank, made out a cashier's check, and FedExed it to Ryan. (No comments, please. I know, I know, but again, hindsight is a wonderful thing.)

70

A couple of days passed and I heard nothing. Then Ryan called.

"Did you get the check?" I asked.

"Oh yes, I did get it finally. I was upstairs when the messenger came and by the time I got down to the street he'd gone. You have to sign for the mail and he took it back to the office. So I had to go and get it there."

"Ryan, didn't you want to say 'thank you'?" I asked.

"Oh sure, sure, I was writing you a note. I'm really sorry. I apologize."

Once again Kathy Levine, registered idiot, made an excuse.

"I realize you must be flustered, after all you're starting work soon so don't worry about anything, just do well."

"Oh, I forgot to tell you, I'm not starting my job till November first. But I'll get the money to you the minute I get paid."

The next day I called Ryan and the number was disconnected. *Now* I was concerned. I called my friend Phil, who's a police detective in New York, and asked him to go to Ryan's house and see what was cooking.

You know what was cooking? My goose! Finally, and I don't know where in this story *you* might have figured out what was happening, the fog cleared: I had been completely and utterly taken, my Prince Charming was a flimflam man.

Phil found out that Ryan no longer lived at that address and in fact had been kicked out weeks ago for nonpayment of rent. Phil figured that Ryan probably waited around in the street for the FedEx man with my check but somehow missed him, and that's why he had to go to the office. He had lived there alone, too, no Tara, no housekeeper, and of course no ex-wife in Atlantic City. His phone number(s) had always been "hot" or some sort of borrowed numbers and that's why I never could get hold of him. He didn't even have a work place anymore; he had left the limousine service weeks ago. Oh, and NYU Law School had no record of such a person and neither did the Public Defender's Office. A little side note: When I told a lawyer friend that Ryan wasn't nervous about taking the bar and that he said he was going to make $60,000 as a starting salary, my friend's jaw dropped. "Are you kidding? *Everyone's* nervous about taking the bar, and Kathy honey, sixty thousand is not a starting salary at a public defender's office, it's more like thirty thousand. You should have known right off the bat the guy was lying."

Bottom line? The whole thing was like a figment of my imagination except for one painfully realistic detail, I was out eighteen hundred big ones. I was really shaken. I panicked and my mind started churning. I spent maybe six times with a guy who could have been anything from a drug dealer to a rapist. I was lucky he was just a con artist who preys on trusting people and plays the game only for money, and plays it so well, I might add, that he fooled the *smartest* lady of all, or someone who thought she was smart. Everything that S.O.B. said to me was calculated and rehearsed down to the first "hello."

I went through some serious psychological trauma because of this experience. I was so appalled at being taken that for weeks I wouldn't talk to any stranger; I was barely cordial to people I knew. My confidence was blasted and no wonder. I couldn't stop going over the events of the past few months and I beat myself up regularly about being such a stupe. How could I not have seen the signs from the very beginning? My God, maybe *he* pressed down the car door lock and purposefully trapped Chelsea inside just to make a scene. And oh, how about my taking him into my friends' house and into my home! He could have snatched jewelry or something. I had so lost my common sense, I didn't think I could ever trust myself again, let alone anyone else.

The few friends I told my story to were aghast and told me I was the biggest schmuck that ever walked the face of the earth. I could only agree. I never dared tell my mother. (She's going to hear about it for the first time when she reads this book. Oy, I mean, Oy vay, what am I saying, I mean Oy vayesmir!)

I was in bad emotional shape for quite a while. Then, one night I was at home and just before I went to bed at around one o'clock I turned on the television and got some talk show, I don't even know which one. On the small screen, a woman was talking about how she had been taken by a con artist. She'd been duped by a doctor who lived with her, gave her an engagement ring, then fell a little short of cash and accepted a $4,000 loan from her. They flashed a picture of this mumzer on the screen and whaddya know, it turned out that nearly thirty other women had been taken by him. The host cautioned women not to go out with this guy or indeed any man who suddenly is "short" of cash. Meanwhile, the victim described how she had become so depressed about what happened, she thought about suicide.

Okay, I lost half as much as that lady and I never thought of killing myself, still, I was as fooled as she. I didn't have a terminal illness; I wasn't put out on the street; I was simply humiliated and tricked. Watching and listening to her made me realize that I was not alone. People make mistakes—some can be deadlier than others, but no one should beat herself up for misjudging character. You shouldn't stop being kind or big-hearted, just be aware of the red flags and when they go up—get out.

In my case I can tell you exactly the places where I should have taken notice. The inconsistent telephone numbers and the business of calling from laundromats and street corners; the fact that he never had a picture of his child; the job's changing dates; the fact that he had no money; the fact that he drank too much. Okay, he had a job and was known to my friend, but credentials are great only if you check on them. The minute the first discrepancy appeared I should have been on the phone. If I'd contacted the law school or the public defender's office, I'd have been made aware that things weren't kosher. I made excuses when I should have been making inquiries.

And what did I learn from this encounter besides the obvious—I'm a shnook, that's what I learned. I'm overly accommodating and in my cockeyed optimistic way, I overlook flaws and try to see the good in people, and in so doing, I filter out the "bad for me" factor. Ryan's drinking and smoking were objectionable. His lack of manners in some situations was objectionable and even if he really had been in law school and even if he did have a future, the truth is I am too mature and settled in my ways to back up for someone who is so far behind. It's one thing to be involved long term with someone who chooses to change careers midstream—you can support that kind of choice. But to start out behind the eight ball is not acceptable for me. So, why all the excuses for this man? Why would I consider settling for so little? Does the recurring theme of low self-esteem come to mind? Those old familiar tunes, "I don't deserve better," and "this is as good as it gets for me" provided the background music until I at last recognized the real melody. Because of the Ryan fiasco, my choices have become clearer. Now, I have a list of *Must Haves* for any gentleman I see and that list includes:

1. Gainfully employed with goals and a realistic financial plan for the future.
2. Strong family relationships.
3. Respect for self and others, women in particular.
4. Optimistic, good-hearted, honest.

We all *say* we want those qualities, but how many times do we settle for the bottom of the barrel because "there's nothing out there." Forget about it! I'd stay alone for the rest of my life with my dog and my friends before I'd sell out to a schmuck like Ryan O'Sullivan again.

4

No-No NoNet, or, Cyberspace and the Single Woman

Thankfully, the next error in dating judgment was not mine. It happened to my friend Fran and I'm including it because 1. Fran's not writing a book. 2. Many of us have done the same. 3. Or, many of us *might* find ourselves in a similar situation, and finally, 4. The world is going on-line and it's new and terrifying territory.

Fran's a computer nut and she's been on the Internet almost from day one. She'd made a number of friends but nothing really special and then she started chatting away with a man who really intrigued her. She and this mystery guy began e-mailing like gangbusters and Fran kept me posted on his letters, in fact she started handing the hard copies over to me. "Kathy, you won't believe it. This guy writes the best letters." I read a few and, to tell the truth, they were delightful, just as clever and charming as anything I'd ever read. "He could be a keeper," I told Fran.

So, they played e-mail tag for a few weeks and sent messages back and forth. She was thoroughly beguiled and really looked forward to these exchanges. She loved the vocabulary, the clever use of the language and the charm of this man. What's more, she continued to have me read them. It was an Internet ménage à trois.

Fran's friend was in sales with a Philadelphia company, and the information he provided let her know she was dealing with a completely solid person. Ultimately the two of them connected on the phone, at which point I left the ménage as they continued their chats for another few weeks. At this point Fran was smitten and she told me that they were going to get together. For some reason, and I couldn't put my finger on it, I sensed trouble. Some of the conversations they'd had, which were repeated to me, made me suspicious. I smelled a

married man and I told Fran my fears. "Get the scoop on this guy before you go any further," I cautioned. Fran thought I was way off, but she did what I suggested and on their next phone call, she popped the question.

"Are you married?" she asked.

His reply? "Meet me for lunch and I'll answer any questions."

Fran reported his answer, and to me, this was red flare number 1. "Wake up and smell the cappuccino, Fran. The answer is right there, the guy's married—with children, bored, horny, the whole nine yards. If he didn't say no, then it's definitely yes. Dump out now, toots."

Did Fran listen to me? In her position, would I have listened to me? When lust and common sense get in the ring together, you know who's going to go down for the count. Fran was determined to see him. Okay, I told her, if you have to meet him, then do it in a large, safe, public place. So she arranged to meet him at the Philadelphia Museum of Art (what could happen with all those Picassos looking on?), and she told three thousand of her closest friends where she was going so that if anything happened everyone would know where she was.

Fran met her Mr. Mystery, spent an hour with him, and then went home. Later she told me the whole spiel. Of course he was married, with children—and bored and "looking for it." He wanted some good old-fashioned discreet fun. Fran repeated his pitch to me and, trust me, the guy was a salesman. "Life is short. Where is it written that you can't enjoy more than one person in your life?" . . . the whole megilla. Oy. Red flare number 2. This road always leads to a dead end, no outlet. I told Fran but she wouldn't listen to reason; hormones on overdrive have no ears and she cruised on into a relationship. It was hot and it was fiery and then came the first Saturday night. He took his wife to the theater and Fran hung out with me, the first of quite a few Saturday nights that she spent waiting for me to finish work. Christmas came and went without a gift or a visit from Mr. Wonderful and New Year's rang in alone. By then, poor Fran had seen the handwriting on the wall in big capital letters: Y-O-U J-E-R-K!

I didn't rub it in, Fran was too crushed, but we did talk about the situation. Sure, the window of opportunity begins to close, but if you go off the beaten path and start looking for someone in the wrong place, you're going to get left holding the bag. If a married guy is coming on to you, this means that he's done it before and he'll do it again. You'll just be another chapter in his book of dalliances and though you might have a wonderful romantic passionate time and think it's something you'll reflect back upon when you're eighty, you have to be prepared for the pain. Plus, there's the fact that you are causing someone else real serious distress. And even if the guy jumps ship, dumps his wife, and marries you, what are you getting? Someone with a lot of baggage and a banner that proclaims, "If I could do it to her, I can do it to you" and now you've simply become the wife who can be cheated on. There are some situations from which you've got to turn around and walk away. And, thankfully, that's exactly what Fran finally did.

She's back at the computer now, a sadder but wiser communicator. I don't know what happened to Mr. Mystery but I'm sure he's found someone else's website to crawl into.

Okay, here's what I learned from Fran's folly: When you start getting older and you feel a bit less desirable, you get a little more worried and it's very tempting to make the wrong choices. Don't do it to yourself, don't settle for less, settle for more. And as far as Internet romances, be a smart (cyber) cookie and stay away from the crumbs!

5

Fun with Fen-Phen, or, Leaving the Fat of the Land

Why did Mother Nature make all the delicious food fattening and all the rest boring? Even a bunny can eat only so much cabbage. Let me ask you something, would Peter Rabbit turn down a piece of carrot cake? I don't think so. As for me, a chocolate bar soothes my soul, a piece of cheesecake warms my heart, and boy, can I ever wolf down what soothes and warms me. Which brings me to gluttony. What a horrible-sounding word. It used to strike terror into my heart and make my blood run cold, but, you know what, as I told you at the beginning, there's been a change in my lifestyle and if that ain't enough, there's been a change in the way I stuff myself. As of this wonderful moment, I'm removed from gluttony. I look at it like something I used to know, something I divorced, happily, and something that, with my blessing, took custody of my fat.

In one way, I hate to start talking about weight gain again, but in another way, I know that so many of us go through this over and over—although not everyone is reminded of it in the manner that I am . . . on the air, in the mail, and over the Internet. Every day I hear about my hair, my nails, my aging process, and my size. My life was a constant battle to keep weight off and I had a thousand generals telling me, via the mail, how to conduct this battle. At a certain point, I couldn't keep ignoring it. I had to address the issue.

When I began on QVC, ten years ago, I was still a "kid" in my thirties and, like all "youngsters" in the predawn of the dietary age, I didn't think that much about what I ate. If I gained some weight, I took it off. If I gained again, so I took it off and so on and so on until I passed forty and things changed radically; it was more on than off. And even though nutritional labels are placed on just about everything but toilet paper nowadays, falling into a box of Oreos is a whole lot more fun than paying attention to labels. For me good nutrition was when I felt absolutely full.

I could put on weight with no problem, that hadn't changed, but it became increasingly difficult to get rid of the unwanted pounds. The old tried and (un)true methods failed. They went something like this. I'd feel bloated and decide that I would take off those few ol' devil mounds that had attached themselves to me. I'd get up in the morning and plan my eating day. I would have oatmeal with skimmed milk for breakfast, a salad for lunch, and stir-fry veggies for dinner. I wouldn't drink, but that's easy for me since drinking is not a necessity—I only drink socially. . . . Of course, I sure love to be social.

I'd stick to the regimen for three days and during that time I was very conscious of what I was putting into my system. I'd back off the damn cookies and would not nosh during the day. After my evening meal at 6:30 or 7:00, if I were sitting at home, I'd have maybe a few pretzels or a cup of tea. I was really careful. I also drank lots and lots of water. And so it went for three days and at the end, I'd lose three or four pounds and my belly would flatten a little bit, my skirt would button better, and everyone would say, "You look thinner . . . in the face."

If you can drop a few, even if it's water weight, you do narrow down and your features get a certain "etched" dimension, like you can see your eyes again. Occasionally I'd stick it out for nine days and drop maybe five or six pounds. Is that enough? Pick up a sack of potatoes in the supermarket that weighs in at those numbers and you'll get an idea of what I'm talking about; it's a load. Look, I could always do this for an occasion, you know, a party, an awards dinner, a date, and because I had a goal in mind, I knew where I was going. That's the problem. Once the goal is attained, you're back to where you can now eat again—or so you think. Believe me, between the dips and the chips, I could gain everything back in one party! As you can see, this method is the opposite end of permanent.

Meanwhile, I tried every new weight-loss method that came along to see if I could achieve a more lasting result. And whatever the method called for I did it. I drank it, I chewed it, I ate it. We've all done every diet program. We're all veterans of the dietary wars, and most of us are walking wounded. In talking to weight counselors I described my eating persona and the best way I could express myself was to tell them that whenever I ate I saw this "pendulum" hanging over me. One side of the arc said "empty" and the other said "full," and I never once saw the damn thing swing over to "full." I'm not kidding, that pendulum was something I saw all my life and I think all people with weight problems have something like that in their lives as well. (Did Edgar Allen Poe have a weight problem?)

At the dining table, I'd eat and eat and still could not get that swinging pendulum to move. I never saw the silo of my body filling with food to the top. I would sit at the table with people my age and my background and they were eating the same food as me but they would stop and I'd go on sucking up the calories. (My middle name should have been Hoover.) I knew I was full but I didn't feel it, the pendulum was dangling somewhere in the middle, the "Hey, Kathy, you need to stuff down some more" zone. I also knew that this feeling of mine was very real and not imagined. There was some damn chemical signal missing that would push the pendulum to the far side and for want of some kind of control, even though I was full, I ate beyond full.

After all those years of three- to nine-day (un)wonder diets, I had gotten into a pattern. The trouble arose when, after forty, the pattern was altered. My body rebelled. One Twinkie and my butt was the size of North Dakota—make that North *and* South Dakota—hey, throw in Minnesota. Whereas once I'd been able to put the brakes on quickly and easily, now it was a drag. I couldn't get myself into the oatmeal, salad, veggie groove for even one day.

With my pendulum stuck on empty, I was always hungry and always thinking about food. What I didn't think about was exercise, and that compounded my problems. It's just like a bank account; you put x amount of money in, the account swells, and at some point you're very rich. Well, I started dumping food into my account and suddenly I was rich in fat, the Chase Bank of Chunk. And I wasn't expending any of this fat either, I was simply sitting on my tookus and doing my job and having a good time. I no longer wanted to look in the mirror. Even shopping, a favorite pastime, was no longer a pleasure or easy. It wasn't about the joy of getting a new dress, it was about the art of camouflage. It was prayers and hopes that every week I could get the zipper up on the new outfit that I bought for next week's party. Things were so bad I didn't know from one week to the next if I could fit into my wardrobe. It got very scary because I was out of control. Clearly this was a runaway situation. This was that bus from *Speed* and Kathy Blob was at the wheel, not Sandra Bullock. I had a renegade problem that wasn't going to get better because I wasn't getting any younger and, oftentimes, with age comes a sedentary lifestyle.

Again, I want to reiterate that if you're large and you're healthy and you're happy that's terrific. But I wasn't any of those things; moreover, the events of my daily life conspired against me. Guests and vendors come to QVC to sell their products and part of my job is to spend time learning about their products and in most cases the class is conducted over a meal. On Gold Rush Day, where we sell nothing but gold jewelry for twenty-four hours, the buyers bring in lobster, shrimp, and chocolate truffles for the hosts. Guess who's the number one volunteer for Gold Rush Day? Soooohweeee. What better place for Miss Piggy to learn about the product than at the trough? Damn it, people just love to meet and eat. I'm forever getting invitations: "Join me for breakfast. Join me for lunch. Join me for tea. Join me for dinner. Join me for a light supper." What is this, a cruise? You'd be amazed at how many meals I packed away in a day. I wish to God someone would say, "I'll meet you on the corner of Madison and Fifty-ninth Street and we'll discuss the product on the sidewalk." How about a meeting in the shoe department of Macy's? Just once, couldn't there be a get-together that doesn't involve food? Fat chance. Ten times out of ten, you get people to attend a meeting because you feed them. To get a host's attention, vendors come loaded with goodies, from snacks to catered meals. An ordinary person says, "No thanks, I've eaten," but Kathy Levine gets right in line. I'm thrilled when they bring food. I'm quiet. My mouth is going but I'm chowing, not talking, so I can listen attentively. Pretty soon someone says it's lunchtime. And off I go to the cafeteria. The clock strikes twelve noon and I've already had three meals. Oy.

Speaking of "oy," something else comes into play here—the Jewish attitude toward food, which is, basically, eat it. Whenever you're having one meal you're already planning the next. (You can always tell if you're at a Jewish wedding because you don't discuss the beauty of the ceremony, you discuss the chopped chicken liver and the Viennese dessert buffet. Forget the bride and groom! Was there enough to eat?)

Well, my Jewish heritage came into play at this time and I couldn't say no to anything on a plate. My focus was "I'm hungry, I'll eat, and tomorrow, I'll diet." I'm not making excuses (okay, I am, but let me, please) when I say that my job and my lifestyle put me in the gluttony stadium and, at the same time, being in the public eye demands that I keep up appearances.

I'm sure I could have gone on stuffing myself right into the millennium and beyond but finally something clicked. What's more, like so many wonderful things in my life, the push came right from Viewerland.

I told you I have zillions of human monitors, people who are always writing to tell me I look good or bad or my hair's funny or not funny, all that stuff. I read every single one of my letters but in general my philosophy has been don't believe your good press any more than you believe your bad press. Then I got a letter from one viewer who really socked it to me. She wasn't exactly mean, or rather I don't think she meant to be mean, but she didn't pull any punches.

"You got so fat," she wrote. "What happened to you? Last year you looked terrific and healthy and this year you are puffy, you have double chins, and when you sit on the air with Joan Rivers she looks like the forty-five-year-old and you look like the sixty-year-old. What have you done? What is wrong?"

What had I done? I knew what I'd done but I wasn't sure what was wrong. I had looked okay during the time I was working on *It's Better to Laugh*. My goal then was to lose enough to make a presentable appearance for publicity's sake and I reached that goal and once that was over, I went out to celebrate. I gained back what I'd lost, plus! My pen pal went on to write that there were new ways to help people lose weight, "wonder drugs" that make a difference in that they make you burn calories faster and take away your appetite. You fill up quickly and don't want more. She told me that she had tried the diet drugs and they changed her life and she was of the opinion that I should find a reputable doctor and see if he could do something for me. I didn't bite. I'm not one who advocates drugs. Having gone through the horror of the amphetamine age, I was not about to enter speed city again. I knew the viewer was trying to help and she did make me think, but I confess I was angered and embarrassed by her letter. I did answer it, though, and thanked her for her concern. (What I really wanted to tell her was to buzz off.)

Soon after this letter arrived, I went on the air with Joan. I was wearing a long white tunic with rhinestone buttons, which was very pretty, and a real short black skirt to show off my legs. Now, I never watch my tapes. I do not like to see myself. I think I laugh like a hee-haw donkey, and I can't stand my profile. Even from a sales perspective, that is, checking to see that I'm selling effectively, I avoid watching because I know that I'm going to pick myself apart. Well, for some reason, I was given a tape of this particular show with Joan and me and that time I watched. What did I see? The petite and lovely Ms. Rivers seated next to a fat, middle-aged, puffy lump whom I immediately recognized as my closest relative, me. I looked like a moored blimp and worst of all, my legs, my pride and joy, my beautiful wheels, were bulging and bumpy. I sat there in my short black skirt with my legs crossed and instead of the sexy gams I envisioned myself having, there were these loaves of challah hanging off my thighs.

Look, I don't want to be a hypocrite, I've said many, many times that weight obsession is cuckoo, but this creature in the white tunic and black skirt now weighed so much over her extended norm that none of her clothes fit. I couldn't button anything all the way. I realized that the way I looked *did* matter to me; if it didn't, I'd go up to two hundred pounds and I'd be fine. But it wasn't for me, it wasn't what I wanted. Hey, I'm supposed to be a role model, not a roll model.

So I watched that tape with Joan and I began to think of the letter from my viewer and then (drum roll) . . . my mother arrived.

As you know, my mother does not pick on me, and has never picked on me, particularly about my weight. When I was the ugliest of ducklings, she made me feel beautiful as she gently nudged me into Weight Watchers. But even my staunchest ally, Pat Seinfeld, was concerned about what she saw. And what she saw was a daughter who was dangerously inflated. She also saw a daughter whose legendary energy was sagging.

I hadn't gotten this way overnight, it had been building up for months. I'd been in Florida visiting my mother and had given my annual party down there, a get-together that's become kind of a tradition. That year it was a double celebration because my book had come out. I went out and bought a new suit; it had a big flowing tunic top, flowing tunic pants, and was a flowing size fourteen. That elastic waistband could have accommodated Dumbo's mother and I damn well knew it. I didn't feel pretty. Florida has humid weather; my hair was bad and my face was greasy. I looked like a big ball of shmaltz. The party was a success. Whether I'm fat or thin, I do give a great party if I say so myself. The party over, I went back up north to eat more and buy more tunics.

Then my mother arrived for her visit and gently, because that's how she's always been, she talked to me. It was never anything like "You're fat" or "You're ugly," she just said, "Kathy you're out of it." That's her favorite expression and it either means I've misbehaved, I'm being obnoxious, or my weight is over the top. In this instance I didn't have to question what she was referring to. "Honey, I hate to see you get puffy." (That's an example of her kindness. I was no longer in the vicinity of "puffy," I was in the realm of airplane hangar.) "Kathy dear, I'm worried about you. You're my daughter and I love you and I'm so proud of you, but I know that your tendency is to go from here to eternity. You'll get lost in yourself and we'll never see you again.

Fun with Fen-Phen

Dear, you're not as young as you were and you have to be careful. Just from a practical point of view, you're getting in trouble. Do you think you can go out and replace your wardrobe in a larger size? It'll cost you a fortune."

These cautionary words were coming from my seventy years plus mother who's up at seven o'clock every morning and is walking four miles on the treadmill at the health club and whose daughter doesn't get up till eleven and falls out of bed saying, "What's for lunch, and where do we shop?" The mother was attempting to give the adult daughter a little bit of inspiration to get on the stick even as she viewed me with alarm.

Okay, here's another little plot to add to the pot. My neighbor Andrea, Chelsea's stepmother, recently had gone through her own weight megilla. Andrea is petite, a size 6, and always had kept herself trim. Then, things happened. Andrea, who's a few years older than I, suddenly found that she had gotten thick and was ruling over a kingdom of cellulite. Proof positive came when she went from size 6 to size 10.

Unlike me, Andrea didn't wait around for miracles, she went to the doctor and under his supervision she dropped eighteen pounds and was closing in on her goal of twenty at the time my mother appeared on the scene. As often as Andrea begged me to come with her, I begged off. She told me that she was taking medication, and that immediately turned me off. I didn't know what kind of pills she was using, but I figured she was on amphetamines. At one time, as I mentioned, I took them, everybody did before they were recognized as dangerous. I had personality changes. I can't afford to be hyper and I can't afford to be nasty and that's how those pills affected me. Furthermore, I was too old to fool around with medications that are potentially dangerous. You can get heart palpitations, you can cop the big one. Plain and simple, I didn't want to do it. I just said no to Andrea. As it so happens, I wasn't saying no to what I thought I was.

My mother went over to my Andrea's one afternoon and had a chat with her. Andrea explained that she was taking new medication, not amphetamines, and that she had suffered no side effects. My mother spoke to my friend from the heart.

"Andrea, you've got to get on Kathy's case. She's out of control and it's killing me to see this pretty girl throwing it away because she has twenty pounds to contend with."

I didn't hear about this exchange till later, but when I did, I recognized the classic Jewish mother construction. Anytime the phrase "It's killing me" is used, you are deep in that territory.

Without letting me know that she'd talked to

Andrea, my mother's parting words after a ten-day stay were, "Please consider what Andrea has done. It's working for her and I really think it would make you so much happier and healthier."

Once the commander-in-chief left town, the brigadier general made her move. Andrea came over to my house, stood in the kitchen, and said bluntly, "Kathy, I'm going to the doctor's office on Tuesday and you're coming with me and that's that!"

Well, I had nowhere else to go; I didn't have any fight left in me and I said all right. So, on Tuesday, I slipped into an oversized jogging suit and went off with Andrea leading the way.

All new patients—there were six of us at this session—were required to go through an orientation. We gathered together in the doctor's waiting room and every one of them had the same sourpuss I had; we all felt like we were in another dead-end street. The doctor walked in and with a quick nod and smile immediately launched into his spiel. No-nonsense about what he said, the doctor did have a sense of humor. He made me laugh a couple of times and boy, was I ever not in the mood for laughing. He was funny, but the subject was serious and went along the lines of, your problem is clearly about food, and one of the ways to deal with it is to write down everything you eat, and drink at least six glasses of water a day. Oy. Sense of humor or no sense of humor, I didn't want to hear this stuff. I began to fidget, my arms were folded, and I was kicking my toe up and down. Talk about attitude! I was thinking, here we go again with another one of the "you've got to write down everything and you've got to drink an aquarium's worth of water." Another diet that's never going to work.

After the doctor's lecture we were taken one by one to have our "before" pictures taken, followed by a comprehensive medical examination, and I mean comprehensive! The health scan covered about thirty different tests, including cholesterol, sugar, thyroid profile, liver profile, coronary risk profile, etc. We had blood tests and EKGs and stress tests. (I liked these tests because I didn't have to study for them. Hey, I've never flunked a urine test.) Then came the moment of truth, the BIG test, the scale. We lined up to be weighed in. I had been told that we would be weighed with clothes and shoes on, so I wore the heaviest stuff I had, that way I would come in at an all-time high. The next week I'd trim my hair, cut my nails, remove my jewelry, and wear a bikini so it would seem that I'd lost a ton. This technique, which I'd honed back in my Weight Watchers days, didn't work. We were advised that we were to wear the same type of clothes throughout the program. Curses, foiled again!

Okay. I weighed in at 164 pounds. At five six and

a half and with my frame, that figure was definitely
an Oy Vay. What's that old saying about never trust
a woman who gives her weight. Well, trust me, I'm
giving it. I know my size 10 sneakers weighed at
least twelve pounds. When I saw that pointer pointing at 164 I just got angry. I wanted to kick the
scale and run. But I didn't. I joined the program—
mainly because I had nowhere to go and also, I
think, because I had seen it work for Andrea, *and*
this type of program was receiving incredible coverage in the media.

Before I left the office, I was asked to write down
my goal weight. I put down 138—a bit on the lean
side for my height, but I wanted to challenge myself
without going crazy. At the end of the program, the
doctor told me I was a good candidate simply
because I had a realistic goal. "You told us what you
wanted to weigh, which was within reason. We get
women who are 200 pounds and five four and they
tell me they want to weigh one-ten or one-twenty
and you know it's never going to happen that way.
They're going to get to a certain point and get
frustrated. You had a good attitude." I know I have
an attitude, so I was pleased to learn it was "good."
I was given a supply of pills and told to take two
little halves in the morning. If they didn't seem to
be working, I was told to call the doctor's office.

By now, I'm sure you've guessed that I was going

on Fen-Phen, the "miracle" pills, which, when taken together, help take off weight. One pill is Fenfluramine, which is from the antidepressant family, and the other is Phentermine, an appetite suppressant, and one fine day they "got married" and became known as Fen-Phen. Like all medication, Fen-Phen has created some controversy. I don't want to delve into the real technical stuff, A) because I'm not qualified to and B) it can only be prescribed by doctors, so you're not going to get hold of it unless you're in the care of a professional. Repeat: This is not a home cure method! Anytime you go on drugs, there is a risk. With Fen-Phen, as with all medical plans, in cases where either the supervision has been negligible or the patient has some existing medical problems, side effects, and in rare instances deaths, have been reported. (Death, now that's what I call a side effect!) Taking my physical condition into consideration, I was willing to take the chance. I do not have a history of heart trouble and the medical examination showed that I was a good candidate. Besides, a minimal dose was prescribed, only half a pill.

Of the side effects other than the Big One, the most significant for me was dry mouth. Unbelievable dry mouth, the kind you get when you go to the hospital and they give you an injection to dry you out. You are parched all the time. This was a bit of a consideration for me, since I'm in a talking business. Drinking lots and lots and lots of water helps. You wind up guzzling gallons and of course you pee all day (and all night) long. You might as well carry a port-a-pot with you. During this period I took more bathroom breaks on the air than vacation time.

Along with the dry mouth, I experienced another side effect. Occasionally, I became slightly addled and experienced confusion. One day I went to the market to get some milk and graham crackers. Later in the day, I went back to the market and bought the same things again. I didn't realize until I got home and saw my first purchases that I'd made the trip twice. I called the doctor and he said not to worry.

"Look," he explained, "there have been isolated reports of memory loss, but as far as my patients can remember, nobody's had any memory loss." (I told you he had a sense of humor.) "Stop the medication for a day or two and then go back," he advised. I did what he said, and it worked. The fog cleared.

When you go on Fen-Phen, you have to decaffein-ate your system, so for the first forty-eight hours I had to stop all caffeine—no coffee, no colas, nothing "dark." Caffeine allegedly increases appetite, so if you drink decaffeinated coffee you're less likely to dip a doughnut or a biscotti in it. Decaffeinating myself wasn't easy. I had difficulty sleeping and oy, did I have a headache! But I got through it. Once I committed myself to the program, I abided by the rules—but I wasn't happy.

At the end of the forty-eight hours I met a woman at QVC who had just lost twenty-five pounds on this exact same program. I sat down beside her and, with tears in my eyes, began to whine.

"Why me? Why is it that I am the luckiest person in the world, I have it all, and this stupid problem really gets me. Why does it bother me? Why can't I just be fat? Why can't I leave it alone? I mean, there are a million women who would change places with me. I have the greatest job. I have the greatest friends, I'm healthy, life is good. Why am I on these pills and why am I always dealing with the same problem over and over?"

The violins were throbbing as that poor woman got an earful.

"You're just feeling sorry for yourself, Kathy. It'll pass."

"It has to pass, I'm so tired of being here again. I'm in the same spot I've always been in. My nose is pressed against the window and I can't get on the other side. I'm always twenty pounds from heaven. I'm just so unhappy. I can't believe I have to give up food again."

Oh, did I ever carry on. Ranting and raving like a spoiled brat.

"It's just the beginning," she told me. "I promise you will feel fine by the end of the week."

I took the pills and I followed the program, which dictated the consumption of 1,000 calories per day from a select group of foods plus vitamin supplements. The doctor explained that, among other things, being on low-fat foods can cause potassium depletion, so along with vitamins, we were given potassium supplements. One reason I liked this particular program had to do with the fact that we were given a list of foods. (Later I did some research, and in the other plans that *I* investigated, patients were given the pills, period, no guides to eating.) The list was spartan but featured foods that would prevent us from losing lean body mass. (Yes, I'll tell you what foods—read on!) Naturally, it omitted a lot of my favorite chows.

And so, with much sighing and little sobbing, I followed the plan. What did I get to eat? My thousand-calorie diet included six ounces of lean meat, fish, or fowl (vegetarians get the proper substitutions); limited dairy products; unlimited amounts of raw and steamed vegetables; three starch servings a day; and two fruit servings. My first thought when I scanned the list was, Forget pasta. I yearned for the good old sixties and seven-

ties diets that stressed low fat and high carbohy-
drate. I had a great time dieting in those days but I
got fat. Alas, I do not process pasta well enough to
include it in my daily schedule. What a blow.

A typical day for me ran something like:

> *Breakfast.* Three hard-boiled eggs with the yolks
> removed. Two pieces of diet toast. Half a cup low-
> fat cottage cheese.
> *Lunch.* Salad, a BIG salad—all veggies and oil-
> and-vinegar dressing. Fruit.
> *Dinner.* Six ounces of chicken breast. Baked pota-
> to. Steamed veggies. Fruit.

I actually varied the diet to suit me and on certain
days I'd go to 1,200 calories to keep my energy up
for work. I usually had three fruits a day and if I got
real hungry I'd have some low-fat graham crackers.
Oh, and I'd indulge myself in the evening with a
diet hot chocolate before retiring. For those of you
familiar with diets, you know that there was nothing out of the ordinary about this one. The emphasis as usual was on healthy low-fat foods.

I hate to tell you, even though these foods are
good for you, you might not be able to stay on them
without a "boost" from Fen-Phen—at least until
you changed your eating habits. The Fen-Phen

made me feel phul-full, and I simply didn't feel the need to eat. I went to the table feeling that I only need to eat a little bit; I didn't want much, and I was able to eat the portions required by the diet. The pendulum was swinging over, and for the first time, my stomach and my head were in agreement. All my Jewish upbringing came rushing back: "Clean your plate. People are starving." I'd be hearing these voices from the past and I just shut my ears. I was thrilled to leave food on my plate. I was eating like a regular person. I was no longer a charter member of the clean plate club.

The first week I showed up at the doctor's office with seven days of deprivation behind me, I got on the scale expecting a plunge equal to the 1929 crash on Wall Street. All I got was a lousy two-pound drop. I was disgusted. I had followed all the rules and only lost two pounds? I couldn't believe it. I complained bitterly to the doctor.

"What kind of diet is this? Two pounds in seven days. That's ridiculous."

He didn't think so. In fact he said, "Two pounds is great. Next week it'll be two more and two more and so on. You just stay with me on this."

I stayed. And in the process I retailored my schedule. I didn't do any drinking and if I went out, I went with Andrea. She understood the rules and knew the restaurants we could go to that would serve us properly with the right amounts. She knew, for instance, that Boston Market serves six ounces of turkey and plain mashed potatoes and plain salad. As you smart readers probably picked up on, the keyword is *plain.*

Andrea and I ate together almost every night and talked about the diet incessantly—let's face it, when we're losing, we women become obsessed with dieting. Andrea was good for me, like a role model. She was only a couple pounds shy of her goal and if I got discouraged, I looked to her. (By the time you read this, we may be engaged. Kidding!)

In the middle of my treatment, I received a generic letter from the doctor's office that said, in effect: "We realize that with the approaching fall season a lot of people are going to want to get into clothes and if we haven't seen you in a while, we invite you to come back. We won't admonish you, we won't punish you, we won't call you weak, we'll simply get you back on track." You know what this letter said to me? It said once the medication is stopped, people gain this weight back and you have to get on the bandwagon again. I could see the road ahead. I'd have a modicum of success and then I'd be back on the wheel again just like a running hamster. I created more reasons *not* to stay with the program but I still kept on. Why? Again, something inside me wouldn't let me quit. I wish I could explain the feeling of not giving up. Better still, I wish I could bottle it and sell it (on QVC, of course).

I had lost two pounds the first week, one pound the second week. Then I reached a plateau where I lost nothing for about two weeks. I'd been on it for a month and nobody noticed any change, nobody said, "Hey, Kath, you're looking good." No fans wrote in and complimented me, nothing was happening, nada.

I stormed the doctor's office and began my litany of complaints. He listened and again answered calmly, "You stay with me. You're doing great." He did suggest that I increase my exercise on the treadmill and stair climbing—not trips to the refrigerator. (I'll be elaborating on my workout program in the next chapter.)

Slowly my mood began to elevate, and suddenly I wasn't feeling so sorry for myself or so angry. I actually could see the window that had been closed lifting, and I could see this might be working. I was held back somewhat because I was too afraid to believe that this might work. Lurking in the back of my mind were the ghosts of diets past. The rebounds back from the lean into the fat, the same old urge to eat taking over. Okay, I was doing great but what would happen when the medication was removed? I knew what would happen; I'd zoom up into my tunics again. Oh me of little faith!

The next week I went to the doctor's office and was shocked when I got on the scale. I had lost six pounds that week. Adding the rest, I'd dropped a total of eleven pounds and was halfway to my goal. What a rush! Being on this diet reminded me of learning how to type. You sit in the class and you place your hands on the keyboard and you're supposed to know what letters are under each finger and you keep going and keep going and you can't do it and then out of the blue "the quick brown fox jumps over the fence" and you're on your way. You can't even remember when you didn't know how to type. Well, that's how it was with my diet. Slowly, steadily, I returned to proper eating habits.

The diet worked, but it took me five months, not five days, to realize my goal. Five months of dedicated, committed, and focused practice of these habits.

During that time I traded fat for muscle. I realized what was happening when I found myself cold all the time. I was shivering in the studio. My hands and feet were ice. Why? Because I didn't have that old protective layer of pudge. So I was cold. Big deal, I could buy a lot of beautiful clothes to keep me warm.

Fun with Fen-Phen

Look, I'd been on a lot of diets before, I tried all the routes, this was the first time that I saw a completely different Kathy. Never before had I seen what I saw and I didn't even know what it was that was different. Then I figured it out. The other diets relied on water loss, and when I was on them I always was on the brink of starvation, just waiting to lose the weight so I could go back to eating cheesecake. I was always denying myself, but in this diet, there wasn't a denial. The pendulum swung over! I experienced feelings of fullness and I wasn't downhearted, either. There is a subtle antidepressant factor in Fen-Phen, and because you feel better you're not as likely to indulge in food. One of the drawbacks of this medication is that many people become resistant to it after a period of time and they have to increase the dosage. This is where you can run into trouble. In my case, I increased for a short period of time to get my desired results and then backed off again. The doctor said if I felt hungry I should take an extra half pill at four in the afternoon. Well, I took it for a few days and then went back to my original plan. I was always afraid. I did not want to be beholden to the medication so that whenever I felt like I wanted a piece of chocolate, I would pop a pill instead.

Here's what I taught myself. If you want a piece of

KATHY IN FEN-PHENLAND

chocolate, eat a piece, just one, and then close the damn box and put it away. This was completely alien to the old Kathy, who didn't eat "one" of anything (okay, maybe that one turkey). I had to finish off whatever I started. I learned to think of food in terms of individual items rather than a collective—you know, one Whitman's candy instead of the whole sampler.

I was burning more fat and developing more muscle because of my increased workout time and what I got was a far, far better figure than I ever had known before, you know, curves in the right places and no detours. Most amazing of all, food wasn't the primary thing in my life. I didn't think about it. Being healthy, feeling fit and toned, and knowing that I looked better than the average forty-five-year-old nourished me. There was no question about my age—my face showed that, but oh boy, my body was toned, healthy, and strong. And that's what made me feel really good. I felt highly energetic, extremely accomplished, and hopeful for the future. I could walk into a room and know that I was on top of my game. This time, because I combined healthy eating with a strict regimen of controlled workout designed to increase muscle mass and drop fat, I resculpted my body. I looked different. I had a waist! I could button my pants and I still get a kick out of getting into my clothes hassle free. The oy was taken out of a major part of my life.

By June I had nearly accomplished what I wanted. I had only two or three pounds to go.

Once my goal was attained, I discontinued the medication but I kept up everything else. I continued to work out and I continued to be mindful of what I ate. It's funny, so far there hasn't been any day of overdoing or binging, nothing like that. I feel that I'm in control. I'm exhilarated and part of my euphoria comes from little things like knowing that if I have a party to attend on Christmas, I don't have to worry—I know my clothes will fit that day. There's something so nice about being able to get on with your life and not have "weight" in the way. It's just not an issue with me right now but I know "it" will always be with me. To this day, I still run into problems. I no longer take the pills regularly, but every so often, when I anticipate a big food day and I know my willpower is more "will eat" than power, I will take the pills in the morning. So far that's only happened one or two times a month. I'm still under supervision, and maintenance includes a monthly visit with the doctor. I accept the fact that I'm a recovering foodaholic and there will always be a fat demon on my shoulder whispering, "Eat that cheesecake."

Among the many obstacles I'll continue to face
are the gourmet food shows that I do on the air. All
the buyers know how sensitive I am about having to
eat yet they have a job to do, too. They come on with
their goodies, chocolate-caramel-dipped apples,
glorious cheescakes, potato chips dipped in peanut
butter and chocolate, and I have to spend two hours
looking at a potential intake of 10,000 calories.

One day I went on the air with a card that said
"Just say no." I had a grapefruit with me and every
time my partner bit into the gourmet food, I noshed
on a piece of grapefruit and everybody in the studio
applauded. But, that kind of behavior doesn't exactly help sales. I couldn't go on shunning the
products and hope that viewers would ignore my
behavior and buy. So I thought, what would a thin
person do on a gourmet food show? Okay, she would
eat her ordinary lunch and would go and occasionally *taste* one of the sale items. She would not eat
everything. She would not polish off an entire
candy-coated apple; she would take a taste. I would
be that "she." Like an alcoholic, I always have to be
careful. I used to worry that the first taste could
send me over the edge.

Armed with my knowledge, I went on the air for
the next gourmet food show, which featured the
"Cheesecake of the Month"—twelve of Junior's
earthly delights, each one representative of a partic-

ular month, like pumpkin for November and eggnog for December. I experienced no difficulty in telling viewers how fabulous the cheesecakes were, that's the truth, and when it came time to sample the wares, I went down the line and, flourishing my fork, "tasted" from each of the twelve.

When I got home, Andrea telephoned; she went ballistic. She'd been so proud of what I'd accomplished and now she was scared that I was going to throw it all away.

"Kathy, I saw you on the food show. You ate everything but the legs off the table. I saw you chowing your way down a dozen cheesecakes."

"Take it easy, I didn't chow my way down. I took a small forkful from each of the twelve and maybe that added up to one piece, but that's all and that was the dessert of the day." (The engagement is off.)

Andrea was so unnerved by seeing me eat, she hadn't noticed that I was using restraint. Moreover, the next day I was back on my program and watching myself. Bottom line, I didn't gain an ounce from the tasting.

So, in a nutshell, that's the story of my diet and the big news about my being less big. I'm still not an advocate of drugs but if you can handle them and if they work for you and you are under the control of a supreme doctor who really knows what he's doing, I think it is an option that can work. If

you are a candidate for the Fen-Phen regime, remember, the doctor in charge of the diet is extremely important. The one I used was wonderfully
supportive, at no time did he criticize or get angry
because I went off the wagon. You need a professional who really knows his stuff and at the same
time is kind. For me, the doctor was just as important as the diet. But, along with his good counsel,
you must do good things for yourself. I had a good
doctor *and* I did smart things for myself. I had to
give up junk food—not just junk, either, I don't eat
much bread and I've nearly cut out all pasta, too. I
now know that Spaghetti + Kathy = Fat. I have to
eat very carefully and watch what crosses my lips.
Occasionally I'll have a potato chip or two, not the
entire Lay's factory. But the urge isn't there as
much either, and it's just so wonderful not to have
food consumption on my daily agenda anymore.
I'm thrilled that I can basically live a normal life,
and the nicest thing is not to have that pendulum
hanging over me. I've learned also that no one who
is trim eats everything she wants. Of course there's
that one in a million you hear about who can pack
in twelve hundred cheese steaks and stay thin as a
rail. There's also someone out there who smokes
four packs of cigarettes a day and will never die of
lung cancer. There are exceptions to every rule.

Your genes, too, have a lot to do with your shape.

As far as dropping pounds, women always get pissed off because men lose so much more quickly than we do. "Hi, I'm on a diet," a guy says, and just saying the words, he loses three pounds. Forget it!

For women it's a different story. When a lady is in good shape and she's in her forties and up, she's being careful. My mother remains a prime example. She does her four miles, and now she's working in light weights with a trainer, and, she's very particular about what she eats. If she's going out to dinner that night she'll have a light lunch. She's careful because it's very important to her to look pretty and good. I guess that's where I get it from. Call it vanity, call it self-indulgence, call it anything you like, it's very important to me to look good.

Interestingly, when I lost the weight my social life picked up. What a pity it is to be judged by the outside, not the inside. But that's how it is today. As I've related, I went out with a younger man and without question my newfound confidence in myself allowed me to date him. Later, my girlfriend in San Francisco set me up on a blind date when I was in the Bay City. I never would have gone out if I'd been the old blob. That Kathy would have been too worried. A blind date was too difficult for her. She was too concerned that she looked puffy and awful. *This* Kathy wore a fitted sweater and a great pair of pants and looked like a million bucks (okay, for you

$950,000). I was confident my date would be pleased. He was, and so was I.

Back at work, I also had a completely different attitude, and that attitude was what people were seeing. Over and over viewers would say, "You have a glow and there's something about you. What's this energy? And how can I get some of it?" Well, I'm happy to share, but I do want you to remember it wasn't only the medication. It isn't just about losing weight, it's about regaining a lot of confidence through strength and power, the strength of your body and the power of your mind.

It's not totally easy for me to keep it up, I admit it. In fact, in my next life I want to be naturally thin. I'm sick and tired of the battle and know the pain people go through.

You asked me to share the "secret" of how I lost weight and I have. Okay, I had to use a crutch. I needed help and was willing to try Fen-Phen; however, I gave a hundred percent of myself and I didn't let the drug do all the work. Hey, it's still hard work and the truth is, this diet is not for everyone. Still, it's a viable alternative for some and for me, it was the answer. I feel fan . . . I mean phen-fantastic!

Extra

Before we leave the Wide, Wide World of Gluttony, I'm going to give you the "diet" that I followed. (I know you're going to write and ask me for it, so I might as well print it here.)

Remember, it's very stringent, and even the doctor said it's probably impossible to follow to the letter if you don't use the medication. It is a good guide to sensible eating, nothing mysterious, and it can't hurt you to follow it—up to a certain point. Bear in mind, *you shouldn't do any dieting without consulting a doctor,* period, the end.

1,000-CALORIE DIET

PROTEIN PORTION	Amount	Calories

Do not eat more than 6 ounces of fowl, meat, or fish daily (or 12 oz. of crab, shrimp, clams, or lobster daily). **You must drink 8 glasses of water each day.**

FISH

Clams	12 oz.	330
Cod	6 oz.	330
Crab	12 oz.	330
Flounder	6 oz.	330
Haddock	6 oz.	330
Halibut	6 oz.	330
Lobster	12 oz.	330
Orange roughy	6 oz.	330
Perch	6 oz.	330
Scallops	6 oz.	180
Shrimp	12 oz.	330
Snapper	6 oz.	330
Sole	6 oz.	330
Trout	6 oz.	330
Whiting	6 oz.	330
Tuna (in water)	6 oz.	180

MEAT (limited to twice weekly) and FOWL

Beef (includes round, flank, chuck, T-bone, well ground)	6 oz.	450
Chicken	6 oz.	330
Lamb	6 oz.	450
Turkey	6 oz.	330
Veal	6 oz.	330
Veal cutlet	6 oz.	450

EGGS

Whole	1	75
Egg whites	3	55
Eggbeaters	½ cup	60

DAIRY PRODUCTS

Cottage cheese (low fat)	1½ cups	330
Skimmed milk	7 oz.	90
1% Low-fat milk	8 oz.	120
Nonfat yogurt	8 oz.	90

VEGETABLES

Serving size = 1 cup RAW or STEAMED less than 5 minutes
Serving size = ½ cup COOKED
Each serving size = 50 calories

Up to 5 servings of vegetables permitted

Asparagus
Broccoli
Brussels sprouts
Cabbage
Carrots
Cauliflower
Chicory
Cucumbers
Escarole
Eggplant
Greens (beet greens, chard, collard greens, dandelion, kale,
    lettuce, mustard greens, spinach)
Mushrooms
Onions
Pepper
Radishes
Sauerkraut
String/green beans
Summer/yellow squash
Tomatoes
Watercress

SALAD DRESSINGS

The following salad dressings are preferred:

Kraft Free Dressings (preferably Italian)
Walden Farms Diet Italian
Safflower oil (2 tsps.) mixed with apple cider vinegar and
    water to taste

Other salad dressings that are fat free and low salt may be
    substituted. Clear dressings rather than creamy are
    recommended.
Balsamic and white vinegar may be used if apple cider
    vinegar is not available.

FRUITS AND JUICES

Best to be eaten raw

Each serving = 60 calories

2 servings daily permitted

	Serving Size
Apple	2″ diameter
Applesauce	½ cup
Apricots, fresh	2 medium
Apricots	4 halves
Banana	½ small
Blackberries	1 cup
Blueberries	⅔ cup
Cantaloupe	¼ melon
Cherries	10 large
Dates	2
Figs, fresh	2 large
Figs, dried	1 small
Grapefruit	½
Grapefruit juice	½ cup
Grapes	12
Grape juice	¼ cup
Honeydew	⅛ melon
Mango	½ small
Orange	1
Orange juice	½ cup
Papaya	⅓
Peach	1 medium
Pear	1 medium
Pineapple	½ cup
Pineapple juice	⅓ cup
Plums	2 medium
Prunes, dried	2 medium
Raisins	2 tablespoonfuls
Raspberries	1 cup
Strawberries	1 cup
Tangerine	1 large
Watermelon	1 cup

BREAD AND OTHER STARCHES

Serving = 80 calories

3 servings are permitted daily

	Serving Size
*Bagel	½
Biscuit	1 small
Bread	1 slice
Bread, diet	2 slices
*Cereals	
(high fiber/low or nonsugar)	½ cup
Corn	½ cup
Corn on the cob	1 small
Dinner roll	1 small
Hamburger or hot dog bun	½
*Macaroni, cooked	½ cup
Oatmeal	1 cup cooked
Popcorn, light	½ cup
Potatoes, baked	1 small
Rice	½ cup
Saltines	4
Spaghetti, cooked	½ cup

---

*Remember: I ate virtually no pasta, few bagels, and no cereals. Grains make cows fat. Cereal is a grain. Use it sparingly if you must use it.

FATS

3 servings permitted daily

Each serving = 45 calories
All fats listed are unsaturated fats

Diet margarine	1 tsp.
Mayonnaise—low calorie	1 tbsp.

FREE FOODS

These items have less than 20 calories per serving. They may be consumed anytime.

Carbonated water (no caffeine, no sodium, no sugar)
    Club soda, seltzer, Perrier, etc.
Cocoa powder—sugar free
Coffee, tea

Nonstick pan spray

The following vegetables may be eaten raw in unlimited amounts:

Cabbage, celery, cucumber, green onion, hot peppers, radishes, and salad greens.

Sweet Substitutes

Condiments:

Ketchup (1 tbsp.), horseradish, mustard, vinegar (apple cider preferred—if unavailable, balsamic or white vinegar may be used)

Nonsalt seasonings may be used.

Extra! Extra!

I just had to add this to the saga of my weight loss. By now, you all probably know that I shlep to New York City for fun and for work and I've been going to my collaborator's apartment for three years now. Over that time I got to know one of the doormen in her building, Manny Reynosa. He and I talked in Spanish as well as English and bless his heart, he was always full of compliments. Latin men sure know how to make a girl feel good; it's a shame

American men are usually too uptight to express appreciation for a woman's appearance.

Anyway, I hadn't seen Manny for many months— in fact, all during the time that I was on my diet program. The new me arrived in New York to work on this book and Manny greeted me at the door.

"Hello, Señora," he said, enthusiastically. Then, looking at me quizzically, he added, "Señora, have you lost a lot of weight?"

"I sure did!" I proudly bragged.

Manny shook his head.

"Well, don't worry about it," he said solemnly, "to me you *still* look beautiful."

Bless you, who love us large.

6

Kathy Schwarzenegger, or, Move Over, Arnold

Okay. I'm on a sensible eating plan for life (!) but I told you that something else figures in with a proper diet in order for you to look and feel your best. I grew up under the wing of a lady who always looked (and still looks!) her best and who trained me and my brothers to put our best foot forward at all times. Ron, Bruce, and I still try to live up to her standards. All three of us are particular about the way we look, although my brothers' approach is

considerably less time consuming than mine—
men don't have to go through the same amount of
work getting ready as women do. Okay, they have to
shave, but come on, that's not such a big deal.
Basically if a man is clean and well groomed, he's at
home anywhere. With us girls, there's a bit more
pressure, and as we get older, the pressure increases. Listen, it's a big deal just getting up in the
morning. After forty, you start rolling out of bed in
pieces and as each section is moved, I hear things
that I never knew could come from a body—
crunches, squeaks, clanks, pops, poops—until finally, I'm on my feet. The toes say oy; the shin says
oy; the back says oy; the neck, you name it, everything is oying. Once on my feet, I take inventory to
make sure all the parts are assembled, and then I
get on with the day. Meanwhile, Chelsea is standing
there looking up at me with a quizzical expression
on her poochie face. What does she know? She gets
up in the morning, leaps off the bed, shakes everything together, and goes out to pee. Me, I'm slowly,
very slowly, trying to get myself out of idle and into
gear and, believe me, each year it becomes more
difficult to shift.

Here's what I've learned. After forty you can't be
lazy about your personal appearance. No more
throwing on clothes, running a comb through your
hair, dabbing on lipstick, slipping into sneakers,

and running out the door—that is, no more of that except when you are off to the gym. And, that's something else I've learned. After forty-five, you cannot be lazy about working out; you've got to get your body in motion. Act like a sloth, you'll begin to look like one, and in case you haven't been to the zoo lately, they ain't pretty.

I always believed in exercise but I never practiced my belief with anything approaching fervor or regularity. I'd go off to a spa for a few days, enjoy the workout program, and then go home and forget about it. Even as I forgot about it, I looked around at friends my own age and older and noticed that while I was turning to mush, they were in superb physical condition. They'd been doing some sort of activity every day of their lives for the past thirty years, not dabbling in occasional aerobics like me. At forty-four, I noticed that Pillsbury doughgirl softness settling in, that Michelin tire around my middle—and it really hit me hard, hard enough for me to pick out a gym and put myself in it three times a week. Just before she started work on *It's Better to Laugh,* yours truly, Kathy Schwarzenegger, took up with a trainer and by the time the book was published, I'd been pumping iron for nearly a year. And all that time, my trainer had been after me. "I can give you muscle," he said, "but the muscle can't show if there's too much fat. You've got to eat right, get rid of the pounds, and let your shape emerge."

I didn't listen to the trainer's advice about dieting but I did pay close attention to his instructions for weight lifting. I was such a jock I even got my own weight-lifting gloves. I became quite adept, too, and I progressed from light weights to bench pressing (I can bench-press 75 pounds). Strength training is challenging and fun and very beneficial, especially for women, who have to worry about osteoporosis.

Anyway, while I faithfully attended the weight-lifting sessions, I wasn't too keen on doing much more than that. Once I started on the Phen-Fen, however, the doctor made it very clear that the program would succeed only if I combined exercise with weight loss.

"If you increase your exercise time, and if you vary your workouts, combining aerobic and strength-building routines, you'll lose quicker and look and feel better."

Music to my ears. The lovely ballad, "Lose Quicker," and that upbeat number, "Look and Feel Better" appealed to me; I wanted to be on that Hit Parade. So I went to my trainers (two brothers, Dennis and Matt Carroll) and threw myself at their mercy.

"Do what you will!" I cried. And what they willed was a balanced workout routine starting with a ten-minute warm-up on the stationary bicycle. I love riding a bike . . . outside. Send me to the board-walk in Atlantic City; let me boogie around a park on a winding path in a rustic setting and I'm with you all the way. Stick me on a stationary bike and I'm kvetching in ten seconds. The seat kills my rear end; the upright rigid position kills my back; my feet fly out of the pedals; my thigh muscles cramp up and scream, *"Fatigue!"* I'm hot and I HATE THIS. I told the Brothers "Grim" my feeling and they suggested that I try music. So I put on a headset and began listening to the lively Pointer Sisters. Well, in thirty seconds I was dying from helping the Sisters through their "excitement." My knees ached, I had charley horses in my calves, my tush hurt—Are we having fun yet? And I was paying for this pain. Oy. Oy vay.

I actually liked the next part of the routine. I was given an overall workout with weights (usually weight sessions are divided and you work on differ-ent body parts at different times, e.g., shoulders, biceps, abdomen, etc. Matt and Dennis said it was a good way to keep from fatiguing any one area. I say it's simply a way to be an equal-opportunity masochist—every part gets to hurt on different days. This workout was designed to give me a feel for weight lifting top to bottom. The weights were very light. The idea is to make the newcomer a winner, to feel a sense of strength and accomplishment . . . to want to come back. I liked it and I went back two days later with my list of demands.

"In six months I want to be able to wear a sleeveless dress without my arms looking like two rolling pins with the piecrust still wrapped around them; I want to be able to wear a cropped top and when I lift my arms and the top rises up, I want something that resembles a waistline instead of that spare tire. I want to walk without the insides of my thighs rubbing together and creating enough friction to light a campfire. I want a tight butt, firm boobs, sexy calf muscles, and a gorgeous, well-defined back." Matt and Dennis smiled. Why wouldn't they smile, they were looking at their next ten years worth of income—solely from me. So I embarked on a most delightful adventure in body sculpting.

I already mentioned that I wasn't crazy about the bike and soon I moved on to the stair climber, and this clicked for me. I found myself climbing like a mountain goat. I was on for fifteen minutes, and then before I realized, I'd worked my way up to thirty. The Pointer Sisters couldn't keep up with

133

me! I felt invigorated, I worked up a sweat, and I burnt up those calories.

In about eighteen months (hey, Rome wasn't built in a day), I started to see progress. Slowly but surely, in the same manner that my weight came off, my body began to reshape itself. I no longer looked like a silo. I had a waist. I'm not a threat to Arnold for the body beautiful title but at forty-five I'm a heck of a lot firmer than I was at thirty-five. Look, to be really truthful, I'd much rather sleep, I'd much rather chat on the phone, hell, I'd probably rather clean the toilet than go and work out. It is an effort but it's worth it.

And so, while exercise is not my preferred activity, I tell you true, there's something real comfortable and comforting about doing it. There's a camaraderie of working out at a congenial place where the laughs are nonstop. Also, if I don't come in, the exercise police (i.e., the trainers) call and ask where I am. I have to admit I really like it and I'd miss it if I had to stop. Anyone in an exercise program will tell you the same story. There's an exhilaration that comes from pure physical activity. Listen, if yours truly can do it, anyone can.

I would like to think that I could live the rest of my life with this attitude, this wonderful health factor that seems really to have taken hold. Even

when I travel for QVC, I take along my sneakers and I find a gym. I worry if I don't exercise. When I had a strep infection, I couldn't work out for three weeks and I was convinced that all my muscle tone would go; the clock would strike midnight, and I'd turn to flab. Well, it didn't happen. I didn't balloon up because even though I wasn't exercising, I was in control of my intake. It was hard to return, true, but I learned that you can take a hiatus from almost anything, including physical activity, and still get back to it.

I know there are people who believe they can't work out like I do. Some can't afford to join a club, others have their time taken up with kids and responsibilities, and still others aren't well. Okay, maybe not everyone can do *exactly* what I'm doing but believe me, you can do *something.* Just get into your sneakers and go into the nearest shopping mall. You can do some pretty healthy walking in any kind of weather, so it's a great way to stay trim as long as you don't stop in the food courts. For my money, one of the best sources for exercise is none other than my pal Richard Simmons. His videos are a great way to tap into exercise.

Richard's the king of compassion. He knows that the larger you are the more severe your problems are and that you may not be able to do all the workouts. His videos are for everyone—particularly the real sufferers. He says, "Turn on my music and do five minutes with me. Sit in a chair and raise your arms up and down. Get the heart rate going a little bit." Jane Fonda and her ilk catered to the incredibly tight and toned. You had to be in fabulous shape to work out with her. Which is fine, if you're in fabulous shape. Richard comes from the standpoint of whatever you can do is good. Just work with me and five minutes become six and six become ten and soon you're part of my program. Whatever he does and however he does it, he does it right. Everybody's Cinderella in Richard Simmons's world.

I started out this chapter by talking about my mother and I'm going to end it with her contribution to this book.

**Stop Kvetching,
Start Stretching
by Pat Seinfeld**

I got up at nine
With errands to do,
Take the dog to the vet
And the park when we're through.

It's ten-thirty A.M.
And I'm still here,

We Should Be So Lucky

Just can't seem to get
The lead out of my rear.

An exercise program
Must be what I need,
I signed up for one
Hoping I would succeed.

I huffed and puffed
With my energy gone,
And that was just getting
My leotard on!

Three times every week
I dragged off to class
To do a tough workout
And reshape my mass.

The sit-ups and treadmill
Got my heart rate moving,
I could tell from the sweat
I must be improving.

I looked like a mess,
My body all scrunched,
But I recovered quite fast
When someone yelled, "Lunch!"

Kathy Schwarzenegger

I worked out for weeks,
Just ate little bits.
Got my weight down okay,
But now nothing fits.

I feel it was worth it,
My weight loss so whopping,
My charge cards are ready,
Tomorrow I'm shopping!

Right on, Ma! We should all look like you!

7

Facing the Music, or, Lending Nature a Helping Hand

After my physical renaissance I sailed along doing my job, enjoying my life, and basking in all the wonderful letters and phone calls informing me how terrific I looked. I really felt so great and frisky and then in early November I received the following e-mail:

Dear Kathy,

I recently read on the Prodigy Bulletin Board that you had a face-lift because management made you do it. I think that would be terribly unfair and I'm sure it's untrue. I hope you'll set the record straight. I know that you only did it because you wanted to, not because you were forced to.

A Fan

Okay, I've already gone on record as saying that in my business, where I'm constantly under the microscope, I am a bit skeptical about reacting to feedback, good or bad. If I believed one set of letters I'd think I was the greatest woman in the world since Joan of Arc, while if I believed another set, I'd think I was the rottenest woman in the world since Cinderella's stepmother.

All people before the public face this kind of intense appraisal. I recently talked to a popular newscaster in Philadelphia and we got on the subject of viewer judgments and how we are so often at the mercy of the audience. She told me that she had been forced to wear glasses on air for the first time in ten years because an eye infection precluded her wearing contact lenses. She got five hundred letters: 250 said "you look great in glasses" and the other 250 said she looked like a "geek."

"You can't win 'em all," I said, giving my standard advice, "and it's probably better to ignore the good reports along with the bad."

I generally take my own counsel and add a few grains of salt whenever I read my mail. However, when the input gets very loud and unanimous, I do pay attention. My viewers are a barometer, and though I would never jump off the bridge if I were told to do that, I do respond to constructive criticism—like I did to the remarks about my gaining weight. Now, however, I was on the line, or rather, on-line, about something more serious than poundage, and, even though only one little bitty letter had come through, I knew that if even a single piece about my having surgery was posted on Prodigy, people would be talking, and soon the story would be out of control.

So, someone had decided that my new appearance was all due to plastic surgery and, *worse,* that I was forced by QVC to go under the knife. Ordinarily, I wouldn't even address this issue, but I do have a reputation for being on the level, and if people thought I was trying to hide something it would be very un-Kathylike. In other words, before someone announces on-line that I've had a sex change operation, I decided to come clean about all my efforts to look my very best. Here's the story straight from the horse's mouth.

I had some words to say on the subject of cosmetic surgery in my previous book. I said then and I'll say now that it's a shame when women get on a merry-go-round of surgical self-improvement. Sure, most of us have some feature that really bothers us and that we'd like to take care of. For example, I positively hated the nose I was born with and after many years and much agonizing, I decided to have it done, not because I thought my life was going to change and that I'd be a more well-rounded person but simply because I wanted to do it.

If you remember, I wasn't 100 percent happy with the results, either—I thought my nose was a bit too upturned. But I was 100 percent happy with the fact that I did it and once my nose was bobbed, I never considered going in and having it redone. In fact, I never thought about my nose again; it became a nonissue and was a done deal. That was twenty years ago and I still feel the same way.

Listen, surgery is surgery, and if you get trapped into thinking that you have to make adjustments all the time, or that you are a "work in progress" rather than a complete human being, you can spend the rest of your life in pursuit of the unattainable. I'm sure I don't have to paint any pictures for you of well-known personages who have become the victims of their own search for the perfect face. That kind of self-loathing is alien to me. I don't care who you are, if your aim is to make yourself look totally different or to become desirable or happy, then you're fighting a losing battle. As far as face-lifts, very often the more you do, the more you look like an old person attempting to chop away the years.

On the other hand.

Many people (many more than you'd think) in the public eye, admittedly (or not) have had a little here and a little there done when necessary. (By her own admission, Joan Rivers has had enough surgery that her ears could meet in the back.) I know some of these people and I always was amazed at their matter-of-fact assessment of what they needed to do and how they go about doing it. I can't tell you how many times I've hosted with a celebrity who tells me that she (or he!) has had a quick nip or tuck and tosses it off as though it were the same as having a haircut or a manicure. Every couple of weeks they're having a snip here or a tug there and they make it sound like a trip to the supermarket. They run in and out of those tucks and nips the way I run in and out of department stores.

While I shied away from anything that had to do

with surgery, right after my book tour I made a decision. I wanted to go all out and make the next twelve months the K.I.Y. (Kathy Improvement Year), a top-to-bottom overhaul. I concentrated on my body and not my face because what could I do with that other than moisturize, use makeup, and pray. My body was different, I could work on it, and I whipped the old shape into the best it could be by doing a combination of workouts and diet. I was very pleased with the results—with one exception, excuse me, two exceptions. After my all-out effort at exercise and slimming, I discovered that my boobs had gone for the long fall.

Joan often comments on how she gets out of bed every morning and hears "bang, bang" and fears that burglars are in her house. Fear not, it was just her boobs hitting the floor. It's a problem that older women have and rather than face it, some get a breast lift or a mastopexy. I'd heard of women who had it done—remember when it was rumored that Jane Fonda had one, or should I say two, and the media went wild because the physical exercise guru had turned to the knife? I knew a couple of ladies who'd had mastopexies, and they were very happy with the results. (I, myself, never saw the end products, I just took their word for it.) Well, I took a long hard look at my equipment and I decided that my chest was kind of droopy and could no longer be described by a word like *perky*. More out of curiosity than a dead-set desire to do something, I went to see a couple of doctors to get professional opinions. Hey, opinions are free. I'll listen to anything, that's how I learn. So I went to Dr A's office in Philadelphia and Dr. A did some tests and made some calculations.

The first step when you're considering mastopexy is getting the statistics; you're measured from your neck line to your nipple—the average length, by the way, is from 16 to 19 centimeters. I think mine were 19 inches—I belt them in at the waist. Then, the doctor gave me the pencil test. A pencil is put under each breast and if it stays in place, you've flunked; it means you have enough sag to hold it up. If the pencil drops, that means your breasts are still defying gravity. I was certain that I had enough sag to hold up a desktop computer, but, surprise, I passed, though I didn't get an A; actually, I think I was more of a B(oob) minus because there was a nanosecond between the placing and the plunging of the pencil. Dr. A was satisfied and said he didn't think there was enough of a problem for him to do anything.

So off I went to Dr. B. Technically, he followed the same procedure as Doctor A.

"No problem," he claimed after examining me. "We can do it quite easily. You'll be high and perky and adorable. And you'll have a scar here and you'll have a scar there," and he pointed to the areas where I was going to have the scars. Not only did I hear about the scarring, I was told nauseating little details of the procedure. Basically they cut the nipples off and set them on a table, lift up the chest, and then reapply the nipples. Great. What if one of the nipples fell off the table and they couldn't find it or it got stepped on? I understand there are newer, less invasive procedures, but my boobs and I had heard enough. I got the evaluations and I made my decision. No way was I going to get hacked up and scarred simply to hoist my boobs. Sure I wanted to improve my body, but I also knew that mistakes could happen. I heard about women who've had mastopexies and wound up with two different-sized breasts or one nipple that's pointing due east while the other is heading due north. Also, you do run the risk of keloids, permanent swelling of scar tissue. I took a look at my sinking chest, weighed what I had been told, and decided to remain status quo.

Part of the reason I backed off had to do with the fact that it would be *unnecessary* elective surgery. My chest is not exposed to the world and therefore who would know whether or not it was sagging? (Everybody, now that I've opened my big mouth.)

And so, I eliminated dealing with one problem. By the way, now's the time to remind you that the assessments I constantly make on my appearance have to do with my professional life. I have to look my best on camera—that is, the best I can. If I weren't on camera, I never would have considered more plastic surgery. My job requires something close to perfection and usually I can get results with something as simple as makeup base. Once I went into another area of topical treatment, bleaching creams.

Besides my face, America sees my hands more than any other part of me. I'm constantly showing rings, bracelets, necklaces, all kinds of jewelry, and I'm constantly handling merchandise in general. My hands get more on-air time than all of Jay Leno and David Letterman combined. Ten years ago, I had the most beautiful hands and nails in the industry. Now I have beautiful nails. Once I rounded the corner of forty, the meno-paws began and my hands began freckling at an alarming rate. I noticed it and I knew that the television viewers had to be seeing it too, especially when I received the following poem in the mail.

Facing the Music

Your hands are old,
Your hair looks like sh–t,
Do us all a favor
And just plain QUIT!

Believe it or not, this heartwarming tribute was signed, "A Loyal Fan." I had to laugh. Oh well, at least it rhymed. Okeydokey, what could be done handwise?

Not much. Hands are the windows of age; you can putchky around with most any other part of the body, but your mitts are the giveaway. I'm sure you've noticed women who've had surgery on their faces and look years younger—until they raise their hands, that is. Occasionally, I work with ladies of a certain age, several of whom are not celebrities, and though they have beautiful young faces, and the bodies of twenty-year-olds, their hands are like chicken feet. And it's not just television personalities who have to accept the hands acting as age giveaways. There are ladies out there who have flawless skin, tight necks, and beautiful (capped) teeth; they're stunning and you'd never in a million years guess their true ages. Those ten fingered babies are the tipoff—the only part of the body where you really can't take nips and tucks. That's because there isn't an appreciable amount of skin to work with, which puts the kibosh on surgery.

Once those veins start showing and those freckles start popping, you are looking at altacockahood. (I know of one exception to this rule, Joan Rivers. She's got the youngest hands in the industry. They're like a twenty-year-old's, snow white and not a vein or a bent joint. I don't know where she's hiding the veins, they've got to be somewhere, maybe behind her ears, but they're not on her hands!)

Bearing all this in mind, I consulted with a dermatologist and she made some constructive suggestions. She told me that I could try special bleaching creams and that for as long as I used them, the freckles would disappear. Okay, I went out and bought the creams.

I don't know if my loyal poet fan noticed, but there was a time when my hands were remarkably clear of spots and that's because I dutifully rubbed in the creams every day, one (a clear gel) in the morning and the other (a yellow liquid) at night. It didn't hurt and within three months, the spots actually had faded. You know what, I liked the results, but I got tired of shmearing myself all the time. So I stopped and the freckles are back, and the veins, which never went anywhere, anyway, have company again. Now I rely on a makeup base to cover the offending blotches. In fact, I rely a lot on makeup base. I use it wherever necessary to camouflage unsightly spots, including my entire neck and chest area when I wear a strapless party dress. It's work, it's messy, it ruins my clothes, it makes me crazy, but it gives the effect that I'm supposed to have—a blotch-free showcase. In my off time, do I bother? Forget it. You like me, you take me—spots and all. And, believe me, I could give those 101 Dalmations a run for their money.

Freckles aren't just a problem on my hands, though. I'm totally freckled and since skin cancer runs in my family, I have to keep an eye out on my epidermis. I used makeup to hide the freckles on my face but as I got older, I got more freckles. Those little spots became harder and harder to hide without putting on a lot of makeup and I didn't want to have my face caked with foundation and powder.

Now, during those months of bodybuilding and dieting as I struggled to get the old carcass in shape, I really hadn't thought about the face. Meanwhile my freckles—okay, enough with that— who am I kidding? We all know that when a freckle graduates from Youth College and goes to Middle-years University, it gets a new name, "age spot"— anyway, whatever you call those little devils, they'd been multiplying like rabbits on my face and were gathering together like a landmass on my cheeks. I saw them, who could miss them? And I also saw other age signs I didn't like; my chin was attending

Middleyears U. along with my skin, and my jawline was turning to Jell-O.

Naturally, I kvetched to my friends and some of them suggested that I do as they had done and have a chemical peel. In layperson's terms, a peel simply does away with the surface stuff and lets the new "baby" skin up. My skin was exposed to the sun over the years and was blotchy but I knew that hiding under the blotch was a pretty good layer of flesh. I do have good skin. My dad has terrible skin cancer, but his mother, my grandmother, had a classic peaches-and-cream complexion, which I inherited. Granted, the cream had curdled a bit, but I still kept my skin as dewy and moist as possible by using the best skin products available.

Alas, there's just so much that even the greatest external application can do when you are fighting age and heredity. My chromosomes began to kick in something fierce. I needed to get back that baby skin of mine and if a peel would do it, okay, I was game. Once again, I sought professional advice.

Some people put a chemical peel in the same category as a permanent wave, that is, they think it's a beauty parlor procedure and many salons do offer a glycolic peel. Also, there are a lot of drop-in clinics, little MacFace Peels, that have proliferated over the past few years offering a quick treatment while you go to lunch type of thing. I wouldn't step within spitting distance of those clinics and with all due respect to the beauty salon, I think you have to be loony tunes to put a delicate chemical procedure on your face in the hands of a beautician. I would not consider using anybody except a board-certified plastic surgeon—and I wanted at least two opinions.

The first doctor I visited looked at me carefully under the lights and after a bit of "aahing" and "oohing" said that a peel would be a good idea.

"That's easy," he said, "but I also think you could use some surgery. Your face is a bit lopsided and I would recommend a chin implant."

I was taken aback. Lopsided?

"Doctor, I don't want to change the structure of my face, I just want to treat the skin."

"But there's so much we can do to *improve* your face. A chin implant will fill out the slack and tighten the jowls, and then the wrinkles would . . ."

The doctor proceeded to take apart my features one by one until I felt less like Kathy and more like Quasimodo. Talk about inch and mile, this was not what I had come to hear. I was interested in a chemical peel, not infrastructure work, and so I bid the good doctor farewell.

That evening I was on air and as usual watched myself in the monitors. Viewers see one scene on the screen, I see not one but three separate views on three monitors, which are in front of me off-camera. The monitors are positioned to help the hosts keep track of everything that's going on. The first shows the full face, which is the one beamed into living rooms; the other two show the left and the right profiles. Isn't it great? I can look into the camera at you and at the same time I can see myself in triplicate, the hair thinning, the freckles popping, and the chin doubling. I get a triple dose of my shortcomings as I sit next to some of the most beautiful women in television. They look three times as good on the screens and I look like the Two-Thousand- (times three, that's six thousand) Year-Old-Man.

That evening I looked at my face(s) and I wasn't thrilled with what I saw. I mean, I wasn't unthrilled enough to think of sticking an implant in my chin, but I did notice that I looked tired and that the freckles were peeking out, and my jawline was slack. Oy. Professionally speaking, I needed to do something to improve my look, I couldn't let this worsen. I also know that if you're going to do anything it's better to do it sooner rather than later. Better to spruce up at forty-five when you're starting to show the signs of aging than doing it at sixty-five when it's going to produce such an obvious difference that everyone's going to notice. Not to mention the fact that it's easier on you because you're younger!

I didn't want to return to the doctor who wanted to "implant" me, so I asked some of my friends whose appearance I admired and got a referral. This doctor examined me thoroughly and quietly, no oohs or ahhs, and said that he would be able to do a face peel without any problems, adding that he did them all the time and the results were consistently good. The doctor did not say any more; the next query came from me.

"Doctor, as you know by my chart, I'm a television performer and really have to look my very best. What would you recommend?" (Talk about loaded questions!)

The doctor looked closely at my face again and cupped my chin in his hand.

"Well, along with the peel, if you wanted, I could do a partial lift on the lower half of your face, just to smooth things out in the jawline."

I was a little put off by hearing the words "lift" and "face" in the same sentence, a sentence that was being applied to me. The doctor further explained that he would make a small incision around my earlobes, pull the excess skin, and suture it off in the front and back of the ear.

I never thought in terms of face-lifting; body-lifting, yes, but I did it through my own efforts and not with any surgical assistance. I told the doctor that while I was sure I wanted a peel, I wasn't so sure that I wanted anything else done.

"It's up to you, Ms. Levine," replied the doctor. "We'll set up the peel and if you decide that you want to do more, just let me know."

I shook the doctor's hand and left.

That evening, I lay in bed and mulled over the situation. Partial face-lift? Me? I took a hand mirror from the drawer and looked long and hard at my visage. Could I launch a thousand ships? Could I launch one tugboat? Chelsea was next to me and she pushed her nose into the mirror.

"Listen, pooch, you know me, I'm as vain as the next woman, should I have a partial lift?"

"Yes," said Chelsea.

Actually, she didn't quite say yes, more like "woof," but I interpreted it as yes.

I'm talking lightly, but trust me, I thought very seriously about what I would do.

Honestly, if I weren't a performer, if I weren't in the public eye, I don't think I'd give it a second thought. There would be no reason for me to "smooth" things out. But because I am on television, I did give it a second thought and a third and fourth. And along with the deliberating, I did some reasoning. I knew that I would be going under anesthesia for the peel; if I were going to do a lift, it would be a lot smarter to go for the "twofer," a peel and partial lift, and get it over with rather than go under anesthesia on two separate occasions. And, practically speaking, one trip to the hospital, one dose of anesthesia, etc., would cost a lot less and be a lot safer. I pondered the possibility over and over. It took me months to come to a decision. In the end, I decided that I wanted to do it and I called the doctor's office and told them to "up" the peel.

Let me make it very clear at this point that at no time, in no way, shape, form, or manner whatsoever did anyone at QVC say one teeny-weeny word to me about getting plastic surgery. The truth is, I didn't even tell management what I planned to do. Moreover, the few colleagues in whom I confided told me I was crazy. The rumor that I was ordered by my bosses to have a face-lift was totally unfounded and completely untrue. My bosses were astonished to learn that I'd made the decision.

So, now you know that, yes, I did have work done. And as long as that's out of the way, I want to tell you about it, I mean *really* tell you. I thought I knew what I was getting into because of all I'd heard from others. Well, I knew nothing. I had to go through personal experience to discover that most people soft-pedal plastic surgery and if you're considering taking the step, pay close attention to what I have to say. I'm not going to pull any punches.

When you go into elective plastic surgery, you're all excited, keyed up, and raring to go. It's not an emergency, like appendicitis, when you are rushed into the hospital. It's something you work and save for long and hard, something you've chosen to do and it's going to make you look better. You're not sick. Consequently you tend to gloss over the risk side and focus on how pretty you're going to be when it's over. In my case I thought only of how glowing and soft my skin would be.

Most doctors stress the upside. Naturally, they're going to be optimistic, after all, you are a potential client. A good doctor, however, will also let you know about the downside, although it doesn't get as much coverage and you tend to hear what you want to hear. Buried among the positives, if you listen carefully, you will also hear the doctor telling you about the risks.

"YOU'RE GOING TO LOOK GREAT. I DO THIS ALL THE TIME. YOU'LL BE FINE IN A COUPLE OF WEEKS."

That's what I heard the doctor saying but I also knew he was mentioning other things, things like: "YOU COULD HAVE EXCESSIVE BLEEDING OR INFECTION AND THERE COULD BE SOME SCARRING OR UNFORESEEN RESULTS. . . . YOU COULD DIE."

Like most candidates for plastic surgery, I glossed over the negatives and embraced the positives.

Let me give you some advice: Don't be a jerk like me. Make no mistake, surgery is surgery, and whenever you start peeling away or opening up, you are at risk. You can have excessive bleeding and you are prey to infection; in fact, you can catch an infection right in the operating room itself. One little germ can come in with someone, jump off, and sit there waiting for you. You're opened and voilà! the germ hops in. Nowadays, surgery patients are cranked in and out of O.R.s like they were orders in delicatessens. Patients are in and out so fast, it's amazing that more of them don't get infections. You can have results that you were not expecting: A nerve can be damaged; you can wind up with a permanently drooped eye or your face can be slack on one side. Oy. It's no wonder the doctors speak so positively about the upside. And boy, oh, boy do they ever talk it up. Nobody wants to hear the bad news, all you hear is, **"YOU'RE GOING TO LOOK TEN YEARS YOUNGER AND YOU'RE GOING TO BE FINE."**

I was full of energy and excitement, convinced that in a week's time I was going to have my beautiful skin back and a clearer, softer image. Man, I was psyched!

I checked into the hospital early in the morning, signed all the papers (the *Encyclopedia Britannica* has fewer pages), and turned myself over to the medical experts. I would stay that night in the hospital and be checked out the following morning. Someone would have to be there to look after me for a couple of days. Guess who looked after me? Of course, my own dear mother, who, I must add, was dead set against this procedure. Then again, she never thought I needed a nose job, either. She thinks I'm beautiful, but God bless her, even though she did not support my choice, she supported me. I explained that I was doing it not because I wanted to look like a thirty-year-old but because I wanted to look like the best possible forty-five-year-old. She was still dead set against it and more nervous than I.

I don't remember anything about the procedure even though I was awake. I was given twilight sleep, which is the medication they use. They don't want you unconscious because they need you to have facial expressions and not be slack-jawed; it's like working on a living canvas. I don't remember talking and joking but I was told that I did. I know I was worried about any confusion in the operating room, you know, all those cases they talk about when people go in for an appendectomy and come out with a hip replacement.

"Don't forget, I'm the face, not the tummy tuck!" I supposedly cried out. And apparently I went on from there. Soon everyone in the O.R. was standing around laughing at this crazy women doing shtick even as her face was being shucked.

The only thing I remember is waking up in the recovery room and feeling like I had a watermelon where my head used to be. I was in pain and on medication. My face burned and felt tight and I couldn't move my head. Suddenly, doubt began to creep in. What had I done?

The night passed and I was pretty much passed out. The next day my mother came to retrieve me and took me home. My face was swollen and an angry red color. When you come out of a chemical peel you look as though you'd been sunburned to the third degree. Not a pretty sight.

The doctor's instructions were explicit: I was supposed to sit quietly, not move around, and periodically put Crisco, I kid you not, on my face to soothe the skin. I don't mind cooking chicken in Crisco, but my face? I was told that big scabs would form and then fall away within two to three weeks. For the next few days that was my big activity— sitting quietly and slathering vegetable shortening on my flesh.

Unfortunately, I engaged in another activity: picking the scabs off my face. (Are you feeling nauseous yet?) I figured I'd help the peel along and with my nails it was pretty easy for me. I began to pick and pick and pick. I was a disaster. My face was covered with bleeding scabs and to make matters worse, the incisions around my ears became infected. This wasn't the "oh, just a little nip and tuck and you'll be on your way" that I'd been hearing about, this was significant and frightening pain. I was bleeding, I developed a fever, and worst of all, my lymph glands were affected. I had terrible discharge from the incisions and I was swollen and sick. I became aware that I had been through major surgery, and that I had elected to put myself at great risk . . . and all because Chelsea said "Yes." (Okay, she said woof.)

I could not stop looking in the mirror and what I saw scared me out of my wits. My neck was swollen so thick I resembled a chipmunk storing nuts for a long winter. Inflamed pieces of flesh hung off of more inflamed flesh that was my face. I was convinced that I was the one in a million who was going to scar permanently. I would look like Little Red Ruined Face for the rest of my life. Oy vayesmir, I was totally panicked, a basket case, and yet that didn't stop me from picking. I persuaded myself that I was assisting in removing the dead skin and hurrying along the process. I didn't realize that I was also peeling off the new "baby" skin. My face was a bloody mess by the time I went to the doctor's office for my follow-up appointment.

The doctor took one look, threw his hands in the

air, and said, "I can't believe you picked the whole thing!" (Or something that sounded like that.) I was certain that I *was* the one in a million who would be forever scarred and I continued to bawl. My mother was sitting next to me and she was a big help, she was sobbing even harder. I was convinced that I was destroyed and the terrible thing was, I had done it to myself. With hindsight, I can imagine how the doctor must have felt. He did a bang-up job and I went and banged it up.

"Why are you crying?" he asked.

"It's over, it's all over."

"What's over?"

"My career. My life." Oy, did I carry on.

If Academy Awards were given for such exhibitions, I would have copped it easily—Best Performance by a Red-Faced Chipmunk in a Supporting Role.

The doctor calmed me down and told me that things would begin to right themselves in three weeks but only if I kept my hands off my face. He suggested I try knitting and if I couldn't find anything to occupy my fingers, he kiddingly threatened to tie my hands behind my back. I promised him that I'd be good and I left his office with my head bowed. My mother made a quick executive decision.

"We're going out to lunch, honey. You need some diversion."

We went to a restaurant and I sat there hiding under a huge picture hat and behind a pair of huge dark glasses looking like something out of *The Bride of Frankenstein.* The waitress took one peep at me, turned away before I could even open my mouth, and forever after concentrated her gaze on my mother. I felt that everyone else in the restaurant was looking at me with revulsion. All the time I kept thinking, "You brought this on yourself and all because you wanted to get rid of a few freckles."

Bottom line? I was supposed to be back on air in fourteen days. I had to take another week off.

I ain't gonna lie. I went through two weeks of hell. Not only did I pick my face apart, the streptococcus infection I'd picked up was incredibly painful and very, very scary. (No one was to blame, but there are a lot of hands working in an operating room and a lot of patients moving through. And I'm sure there were plenty of germs on my own hands when I was picking at those scabs.) I was humbled to the point where I will never again soft-pedal any kind of surgery or toss it off with an "Oh, it's just a nip and tuck."

Don't ever think you can walk, or rather be wheeled, into an O.R. without the possibility of an unexpected unpleasantness cropping up. Face it, you run the risk of infection anytime you go into a surgical procedure. And it can be the most insignificant piece of business, too. A friend of mine went in to have a tiny little mole removed and picked up a whopper of a strep infection just like that.

For a while I was in emotional as well as physical pain and I drove my poor mother crazy with my wailing. I couldn't heal fast enough. Eventually, the antibiotics kicked in and I stopped picking and within about two weeks the baby skin began to reveal itself. I began looking in the mirror again and not recoiling in horror.

In the early weeks, I had to use tons of makeup and pull my hair forward like a sheepdog to cover the redness and scars. I guess that's when that "fan" saw me and sent the e-mail. Now, I'm back to "normal," the only difference is I don't have to pile on the makeup. I wanted to return to the beautiful skin waiting patiently under the freckles, aka age spots, and by golly I did. It's glowing and beautiful and my jawline is tighter and more defined. The whole package came together, but I paid a price.

My whole life had flashed before me in those days of torture. I really thought I might not recover aesthetically, emotionally, or physically. Funny, now that the business is over, I'm hearing horror stories for the first time. Not "oh, it was a piece of cake" but the tales of people who don't slide in and out of surgery. I was told about one woman who went in for a tummy tuck, developed septicemia (blood poisoning), and nearly died.

So, if you decide that you want cosmetic surgery, fine, but go to the best doctor you can find. Be aware that you are as susceptible as someone going in for a transplant and remember too, anyone who undertakes surgical procedures has to have a very strong attitude. (Oh, and it sure helps if you're a good healer and a nonpicker.)

Plastic surgery? It's long and it's tough and don't let anyone sell you a bill of goods on the joy. There is no joy. I was so burnt by my experience that for months I didn't want as much as my fingernails trimmed. Would I do it again? I am delighted with the results, the outcome was beautiful, but I'm definitely not looking for the next piece of surgery to do. I'm going to keep myself looking good by eating healthy and working out. My next book will not have another procedure to discuss.

On the other hand.

What about hair implants? Now there's something I could use. Knowing me, though, my implants probably would be having bad hair days even as they were being plugged into my scalp. Oy.

8

Love and Loss

Something terrible happened in 1996, something that so upset me that for months, sadness and anger took over and got in the way of my usual behavior. As you know, I tend to look at the bright side of things, the cockeyed optimist business, and generally speaking, on those occasions where I do get upset, I pout, I stamp my feet, I go shopping, I feel better, and I get over it. I don't tend to harbor hostility, I'd rather look at the fun side, but this time I couldn't get rid of my rage—that is, I couldn't do it by myself—I had to get help.

As I mentioned in the Foreword, one of the downsides of aging is recognizing your own mortality as well as that of your peers. It ain't easy and there's no sugarcoating the condition, it sucks. Unfortunately, I'm sure that all of you have been or will be exposed to similar situations. Still, it's comforting to know that in times of deep despair, you are not alone, and for that reason I'd like to share my experience with you.

On October 25, 1996, I was on my way to New York City to work on this book. I had the day off and grabbed the opportunity to get some more of my thoughts down on paper; plus, I love any excuse to visit Manhattan. I had to make only one little detour, a quick stop in Philly to appear with Wally Kennedy, host of a popular local TV show, *A.M. Philadelphia,* in conjunction with one of QVC's big talent hunts. We're always looking for the next Bob, Mary Beth, Steve, Jane, or Judy and we do these massive searches periodically where anyone who wants to be a host is given the opportunity to try out. It's always a madhouse, like a theatrical cattle call, and this time was no exception. Between 1,300 and 1,600 people were lined up at six in the morning and every single one of those people wanted to get on the working side of the camera. Groups of aspirants are herded into a room and individually given the once-over. Whoever passes goes into the next room and so on. If you survive the initial weeding, you get a chance to audition and although it's really a million-to-one shot, if someone gets hired it becomes a major media event.

While I was being interviewed on air about being a host, the hopefuls were auditioning and the camera cut back and forth between me in the studio and the mob of QVC host "wanna-bes" at the auditions. I had a lot of fun with Wally Kennedy and when it came time for me to leave, I was really buoyed up. I left the studio, went to the parking lot, and got into my car. I planned to drive to the Thirtieth Street train station, park, and catch the Amtrak to New York.

The first thing I did when I got behind the wheel was to activate my car phone and check for messages. My job dictates that I be in constant touch with my answering machine and I regularly call in every two or three hours to make sure everything is okay. Sometimes I learn that everything isn't okay—I may have to replace an ailing host or make an unscheduled personal appearance or something else—the main thing is, I have to keep in touch. So

I punched in the numbers, heard that I had one new message, and, muttering a prayer that I would not be called in to work, I listened to the recording.

"Kathy, this is Cheryl. I have something important to tell you. Please call me immediately."

Cheryl had worked with my ex-husband, Jay, in the insurance business and I dealt with her from time to time. The message was brief and I detected a note of urgency; Cheryl's voice was shaky. We were friendly but I knew if she was calling it wasn't to tell me about a sale at Bloomingdale's. Immediately I dialed her number.

"Cheryl, it's Kathy. What's up?"

"Kathy, Jay's had a heart attack and he's in the hospital."

"What hospital?" I asked.

She told me and I hung up and called information to get the hospital number. I did everything automatically, without even pausing to think. I didn't want to think.

I got through to the hospital and when I asked about Jay Levine, I was told he'd been discharged. I felt so very relieved and finally was able to draw a deep breath; I'd been trembling since I spoke to Cheryl. I really wanted to talk to Jay, but much as I yearned to hear the reassuring sound of his voice, I couldn't call him at his home. Jay Levine and I had been divorced for ten years. He'd remarried very happily shortly after our separation and had the children he so yearned for—two darling girls. Jay was a totally devoted husband and father, and yet our relationship had continued—not romantically, that was over—but the friendship, the care, the affection, none of that had been affected by our divorce. Jay handled a lot of my financial business, including my insurance, yet I never called his house; it would have been out of place for me to disturb his wife at their home even for business reasons. Eager as I was to speak to him I felt constrained. Oh well, he was okay and that was the important thing.

I called Cheryl back.

"Good news. I just spoke to the hospital and Jay's been discharged. He must have had heartburn. You know Jay and his garbage-can eating habits. He probably ate some enchilada and it sat wrong. He must be at home now and he's probably raiding the refrigerator even as we speak."

Cheryl was as relieved as I and promised to let Jay know later on that I wanted to talk to him.

I got on the train to New York and when I arrived in the city, I checked for my messages again. Cheryl had called and my heart sank at the sound of her voice.

"Kathy, Jay's not home. He was transferred to another hospital. He *has* had a heart attack. Call."

I did call, but not his home. I called his sister Andrea, with whom I've always had a very strong relationship. Andrea's husband, Gary, answered the phone and told me that Jay's wife had brought the children to stay with him while she and Andrea went to the hospital.

"What's going on?" I asked.

"It's very bad, Kathy. He had a major heart attack and they have him on the table. They're doing a cardiac catheterization, which will show how severe the blockages are, and they'll take it from there."

I thanked Gary for the information and told him that I would get in touch later. I hung up the phone and tried not to think.

Everything seemed so unreal. Even though I had been anticipating something like this to happen for years, the actuality was shocking. I say "anticipating" because Jay didn't take care of himself, he was a good thirty pounds overweight and didn't exercise, and his diet was just about pure junk. And to complicate matters further, Jay's father had dropped dead of a heart attack at the age of fifty-two, Jay's exact age—a bad scenario.

I wrote a chapter about Jay Levine and me in *It's Better to Laugh* and so many readers were so moved,

173

impressed and, yes, even inspired by the story of our marriage and its dissolution that I'm still getting letters. I was one of the lucky ones who maintained a very solid, affable relationship with her ex, and now my beloved friend had been stricken.

My mother and father were crazy about Jay; in fact, when I announced that I was getting a divorce, I thought my mother might give me the boot and take him. Of course she didn't but she never stopped loving him like a son and I swear to this day I don't think she understands why I chose to leave him. Thinking about my mother, I realized that I had to call and let her know what had happened. (There was no need to notify my father; he's in a nursing home and in his own world, unable to understand most communication.)

My mother gasped when she heard the news and immediately wanted to fly up from Florida. I discouraged that; she'd just been here and besides, even if she came, she wasn't going to be able to see Jay; they weren't related anymore. I told her I'd keep her informed and she said she'd sit by the phone until she heard from me.

Jay in the hospital. I almost couldn't believe it myself. He'd been in one before, though, just after we were married, when he was found to have

Hodgkin's disease. After surgery he went through the tortures of chemotherapy, and all that time, I'd been there with him, making him laugh and urging him toward life. I wanted to do it again. My fingers itched to pick up the phone and call him. First I'd bawl him out for letting himself get so run down and then I'd make him laugh his way back to health. I'd done it before, I could do it again. I wanted to talk to him one more time because I had such a bad feeling about this. "Don't you go, you son of a gun," I wanted to yell at him. "Don't you dare. My insurance policy needs to be looked over." I wanted to call and connect with him because of this terrible feeling that I might not see him again. But I couldn't, he wasn't my husband.

There's a tremendous push and pull when you are the other woman, and I was the other woman. The game was over and I had no privileges. And so while part of me said, pick up the phone, this could be your last chance, the other part said, get out of the way, he ain't yours, just pray for him.

Almost without realizing it I slipped back into memories and found myself going over old times, the hurts and grievances as well as the fun. As most of you already know, I came to the point where I felt I had to move on. It was a terrible time but Jay and I carried integrity through everything and were very communicative. Sure, things could have taken a nasty turn especially during the divorce proceedings when the question of assets arose but that wasn't my interest. I didn't want Jay's money, I wanted his friendship, and I got it—for twenty years.

For a while Jay would call every day to see how I was, then after my job took hold and after his marriage, the calls became far less frequent. We remained in touch, though; I was one of very few divorced women who still have a lot of the ex-husband in their lives. Some people could misconstrue what I'm saying and try to put a spin on it, but we weren't doing anything other than being loving, caring friends.

Jay never stopped looking out for me, and as a result, he was in my life not for ten years but twice that. I really relied on Jay and leaned on him, and you know what? I learned that no man could ever be counted on the way that man could. In all the years I've been single, I've never found anyone who was as concerned about me or who had it together the way Jay did. The men I dated had baggage, an ex-wife to contend with or screwed-up kids, or a demanding mother, all the barnacles that can cling to a middle-aged guy and sink him. I guess what I'm trying to say is that everybody seems to have something whereby their interests are taken back to their families, but though no one was more interested in his family than Jay, he had the ability to take care of a host of people without anyone feeling shortchanged. He was the best son, the best brother, the best husband, the best ex-husband, the best father, and the best friend, and we all relied on him. Jay Levine was a mensch.

Jay was so proud of my success. Within two years of our divorce, QVC was touted as one of the fastest-growing companies in the country and I was growing with it. People were talking about this crazy shopping show and this funny lady. I was the flavor of the month and once in a while Jay would call to regale me with stories about my popularity.

"Boss"—he gave me that nickname early in our marriage—guess why—"I was at the bank today and when I signed my name the teller asked, 'Are you by any chance related to that lady on TV?' And I said, 'Yep, I'm her ex-husband.' And the next thing you know, the entire place was buzzing. People were pointing to me and saying, 'That's Kathy Levine's ex-husband.' Can you beat it? I'm a celebrity."

Jay didn't have an ounce of sour grapes in him; he was thrilled and proud of my achievements and, bless his heart, he wasn't above using them to his own advantage. My name became a sort of entree for him and helped to break the ice in certain situations. He'd walk into an office and strike up a conversation with the secretary, a conversation that invariably led to a discussion of cable television and the QVC network and then it was "Do you ever see Kathy Levine? She's my ex-wife." Jay said that my name often was an open sesame for him and I was delighted.

Jay had gone through a bit of a rough patch; the hide business that his family had been in for years kind of dried up, and in his late forties, when most guys are looking forward to retirement, Jay switched careers. He wanted to make sure that his wife and children were provided for properly and after weighing the rather limited choices available to a man his age, decided to go into the insurance field. In 1993 he started in his new business at a level far lower than the one he once held; he went from being CEO to entry level. Jay was told that it would take five years to build up a clientele and the going would be tough yet he thought he could do it.

"I'm going to do fine, Boss," he told me, "but boy it's a bitch getting started."

Jay was under unbelievable stress yet he never complained. Selling insurance is a heck of a profession; you have to pound the pavements and even though everyone needs it, everyone hates the thought of paying out money for something that's totally ambiguous. Young people are skeptical because they think they're going to live forever and older people who have insurance don't particularly want to make changes. Nobody thinks about disability that much except for people like me; I make my living on my voice and I need my money. I was clear about getting insurance but I'm the exception. Poor Jay had to overcome a lot of resistance. I gave him lists of potential clients and I also highly recommended him to my colleagues. When you're investing in something like insurance it's important to know that you're dealing with someone of absolute integrity, and knowing Jay as I did, I felt no qualms about giving my imprimatur. I was glad to give something back to him and he appreciated it, too. I'd been receiving his largesse for years; it was a pleasure to reciprocate.

So Jay was very much in my thoughts all that day in New York City. The afternoon was taken up with the book (or rather, trying to write with all that was going on) and then in the evening I planned to have dinner with my brother Ron, who had come up from Florida, and some friends. Right before I joined the gang at the restaurant I called Gary to get the latest and was told that the catheterization had revealed a quadruple blockage. Jay was going into a quadruple bypass under emergency conditions. I have to admit I did not have a good feeling about this. Again, Jay's physical condition scared me, he was just so out of shape. I mean, instead of going to play basketball, which he loved to do, or exercising in some fashion, he usually went to see his two darling daughters participating in their activities. So there was a lot of sitting and a lot of lunching because that's what you do when you're a daddy and when you're in business. Jay got puffier and puffier and started to get the pasty look of someone who isn't well, someone who's a prime candidate for a heart attack. And then there was his attitude; he walked around *expecting* something to happen.

"Yeah, I've got a bad heart," he'd say. "My old man had one. Got up one day, had lunch, and dropped over dead. I'll probably be just like him."

It was such a self-fulfilling prophecy—my father had one, I'll have one, and he literally waited for "the big one." Once he told me that if he dropped dead at least he'd taken enough insurance to know that his family would be okay.

"That's a stupid thing to say, Jay," I barked. "You have children. You want to see them grow up. You want to see them graduate from college. They don't want to see an insurance policy paid out, they want to see their father. Take care of yourself."

180

"I know, I know," he answered, and then he reached for some candy or some potato chips or anything that spelled trouble.

Jay was a closet eater who came out, ate, and then ran back into the closet. He'd have a doughnut in the morning and then say that he didn't have any breakfast. In his mind, doughnuts didn't count. He'd have a double cheeseburger for lunch, a heart attack on a plate to begin with, and if you asked him what he'd eaten, he'd say, "Oh, just a hamburger." I remember him telling me he'd done pretty well on a stress test except that his triglycerides were a little high. "How high?" I asked. "Oh, about three hundred," he answered. Well, that's about a hundred points more than they should have been.

There were so many indications that Jay wasn't handling himself well, but he always made excuses and the biggest excuse was that he was too busy working to pay attention to his diet. As if that weren't bad enough, he wasn't getting proper rest either. He said that he couldn't sleep well because his mind was racing to come up with new names, new sources to increase his business. Furthermore, he was still working hides on the side for extra pocket money. If someone needed a load of skins, he would broker it and take a commission. Look, he wasn't that different from a lot of guys except that he was a little bit old to be involved with a new business and a young family. He was doing what most men do in their thirties.

I got to the restaurant and told my brother the news. Ron blanched. "I knew it would happen," he said. "I just knew it." Yes, we all knew, but no one could do anything with Jay. The only one who could do anything was Jay himself and he wouldn't accept that responsibility.

Before the meal, we drank a toast to wish Jay well and then proceeded to eat. I must say my appetite was not affected, although my social sense was. Another time I would have been much more involved in what was going on around me; celebrities galore were packed in front of the bar and I spotted Elizabeth Hurley and Stephanie Seymour, the Victoria's Secret girl, both of whom appeared to be seven feet tall and seven inches wide. But I wasn't in the mood for star spotting; it was enough to get my meal down.

Prior to boarding the 11:30 train, I called Gary again. He was very subdued. "It's not good, Kathy, it's not good. His blood pressure is dropping and it's critical. He's on the table but the heart is so severely damaged that they're thinking the only hope is a transplant. They're going to leave him open and see how he does."

"I'll call you when I get home," I told Gary.

I really wasn't thinking straight. I wouldn't get home until very early in the morning and I wasn't about to bother Gary then. I did call my mother from the station to give her an update. I told her to go to bed and I'd telephone as soon as I heard anything else.

It was almost two in the morning when I got home. There were no messages and, hoping that no news was good news, I did not make any calls. I had to go pick Chelsea up at my neighbor Andrea's house. I stood there in my kitchen and composed a note to Andrea saying that Jay had had a massive heart attack and was in critical condition. "Keep your fingers crossed," I wrote. I took the short walk to Andrea's place, opened the door, picked up my pooch, and put the note on a table. I looked up at the clock; it was ten minutes of two. I kid you not, but a funny feeling came over me and I remember shivering as an icy wave ran through my body. I walked with Chelsea for a few minutes and then returned home. I got into bed and spent a restless night.

The phone rang at twenty after six. Now, there would be only two reasons for my phone to ring at that hour: to tell me about my father, whose life really had been over for years, or because of Jay. I knew it wouldn't be the call of choice. I knew it wouldn't be my father, I just knew. I picked up the receiver.

"Kathy, it's Gary. It's over."

I find it amazing that I talked to Gary and remembered what he said and all the time it seemed like a dream, a very, very, bad dream.

Apparently Jay had had such a severe heart attack that by the time he got to the hospital it was too late. It wouldn't have mattered what they did; his heart was out-and-out destroyed.

"He was dead for about ten hours but they kept him on the resuscitator to see if they could get a pulse." Gary spoke wearily. "They disconnected the machine at ten of two this morning and he went instantly." Ten of two, the exact time that inexplicable chill went through me.

There was nothing more to say to Gary. I thanked him for letting me know and put down the receiver.

Jay was dead.

I had never lost anyone so very special, I mean a contemporary. My grandmother was old and she was "supposed to die" and there was a close friend of the family whom I called "aunt" and she had a lengthy cruel illness before she died, but she too was older. This was the first death in *my* generation and I didn't know what to do. I thought of Jay's mother and how much she loved him. She loved all her children, but Jay was the sunlight of her life; he was special. I was grateful that she wasn't here to see this. Anyway, no parent should live to see a child die. So there I was in my bed and all I wanted to do was talk. My first thought was to call my mother, but I thought better of it. I didn't want to rouse her so early, I wanted her to have a little more time not to be upset.

I have one girlfriend, Irene, who gets up at six every morning because she has to appear at her job at seven. She was the first person I called. I had my first cry with Irene. I'm not really good about falling apart in front of people but I'm comfortable with Irene. Oddly enough, the next person I spoke to was a man whom I had just met. We'd been on one date and I knew virtually nothing about him except I got the feeling that he would be available to me emotionally. Of all the people I could have called, for some reason I called this new person in my life—partly I think because he'd told me he was an early riser and got to work at 6:30. I beeped him and my call was instantly returned.

"Honestly, I don't know why I'm bothering you," I said tearfully, "but you're someone I wanted to talk to. I wanted you to know that my ex-husband died." He said he was so sorry and spoke soothingly and sweetly. I was kind of taken aback when he added that he knew how special Jay was.

"How do you know Jay?"

"You talked a lot about him on our date."

"I talked about him?" I said.

"Yes, you told me that when you're seeing some-one seriously you always arrange for your ex to meet him. You told me that he had good taste in men and looked out for you. He sounded like a great guy and I'm truly sorry I will never get to meet him."

I burst into tears. I guess Jay was so ingrained in my system, I spoke about him without even realiz-ing it. My friend let me bawl a bit and then asked if I wanted him to come over and spend time with me.

"Oh no," I answered, "of course not. I mean, thank you but I really don't know you that well. But thank you, thank you."

Can you believe it? I beep this guy early in the morning, pour my heart out, and then tell him I don't know him well enough to have him come over. I'm sure there was some sort of logic to my thinking but I haven't figured it out yet. Later in the day, he sent me flowers with a note saying, "I'm here if you need me," and I have to say it meant an awful lot.

I called my best friend, Phyllis, my oldest friend from my married days. When I left Jay, she was practically the only person in our group of friends who stood by me. "I think you're crazy to leave that wonderful man, but you're my friend," she declared. Phyllis didn't judge my action and divorce me like the others did. I think that's the sign of a true friend, someone who may not agree with what you do, but doesn't dump you for doing it.

Phyllis and I had a long cry over the phone. We talked about Jay and about how great he was and how we'd both like to kill him for dying. Boy, it's amazing how you can go after someone who's died relatively young. I blamed Jay for "letting" himself die—like he wanted to! I suppose I was plain old frustrated at not being able to "change" him. Nobody was going to change Jay Levine, not me, not his wife, nobody.

At the end of our crying fest, Phyllis told me that she would let me know about the funeral arrangements. She invited me to sit with her and her husband.

"You'll have to sit with us," she said. "Nobody else is going to want to sit with you." She was right. I was kind of a pariah with certain persons. I no longer saw some people I had known in my married days who hadn't forgiven me for divorcing Jay.

My next call was the one I dreaded most. I had to call my mother. What can I tell you? She was so sad, so terribly sad. Again, I insisted that she not make the trip up. "It's too much. You've just been here. You've got to stay with your husband. Jay would understand, he wouldn't want you shlepping up

here." I convinced her that I was right and promised to call and tell her all about the services.

Jay died on a Friday. According to the Jewish
religion, the dead are to be buried A.S.A.P., which
usually means the very next day. It's not a hard-
and-fast rule anymore because families are usually
scattered and it takes time to gather everyone
together. You're permitted to take as long as you
need, but most often the body will be put in the
ground within forty-eight hours. The rites are very
simple and basic. There's no embalming; the body
is washed and cleansed, covered with a simple
shroud, and placed in a simple pine box. We don't
do the makeup or the posturepedic casket; you go
out the way you came in, as plain as possible. The
exception to the rule of "in the earth within forty-
eight hours" occurs when, like Jay, a person dies
on a Friday. Again, according to Jewish tradition,
burials are not done on Saturday, the Sabbath.
Actually, neither are weddings (until sundown).
The Sabbath is supposed to be kept holy and free of
added ceremonies. So, Jay's funeral would take
place on Sunday and I would be there. There was no
doubt in my mind that I would attend; however, I
did have doubts about how I should handle it—I
wanted to make sure I didn't commit any breaches
of etiquette. I knew my place and would keep it.

Love and Loss

Since I was scheduled to be on air that weekend, I figured that I'd go to work on Friday and Saturday and just ask for Sunday off.

I had made all my early "talk and cry" calls and at nine o'clock I began the business ones. Having had the opportunities to release my emotions, I felt a lot more in control. I knew there must be a grieving process, but I just wasn't quite sure what it would be like. Shortly after nine I called Mary at QVC.

Mary handles the host scheduling and is a wonderful person. She manages twenty-two whining animals and at no time is one host not sick, another not in the mood to work, or one simply not coherent. Mary is always juggling hosts in the air to maintain a live show. She goes through hoops and no matter what the situation, there's always one kvetch, one crier, one bruised ego who complains, "Why do I have to go on at two in the morning? What did I do wrong?" Poor Mary is always soothing egos. She has the worst job in the world and she is the best. We all love her. Feeling totally composed, I dialed Mary's extension and when she picked up, I spoke, I think in one breath.

"Hello Mary this is Kathy I know you don't know that much about me but my ex-husband was my very dear friend and he dropped dead this morning and I can work Friday I can work Saturday but for the funeral Sunday I'd like the night off thank you."

Her reply was quick. "Of course, Kathy, we'll take care of everything, don't worry."

When I heard that, I started crying. She was so nice to me, I couldn't handle it.

"Don't worry, Kathy, everything will be settled. Don't worry, I'll take care of it."

I thanked her again and hung up. I couldn't believe that I'd so lost control. It was Mary's fault for being so sweet. I'm not used to being treated so gently and kindly. Don't get me wrong, I mean, it's not that I've been cruelly treated, I've just not been in a position in my life where I've asked for a lot. I don't like to ask for things. When it's my job and my commitment, I like to do what I'm supposed to do. I don't want someone else to have to do it for me.

Shortly after the call to Mary, my phone rang, and when I picked it up I heard my boss Jack's voice.

"Kathy, I just heard the news. I am so sorry. We've taken you off the air tonight." That did it! The floodgates loosed and I was bawling.

"No, Jack, I really want to work. It's weekend and Mary Beth never gets time off with her children, and poor Steve always gets called in for the music items. . . ." Doc Severinsen was coming in on Saturday and I was supposed to work with him. If I didn't make it, I was sure Steve would be tapped. "I know you're going to make Steve come in and he's going to hate me and . . ." I was blubbering like a baby. "I can do Friday. I can do Saturday. Honest. I just need Sunday." Now all this was said through gasps and sputterings.

"Kathy, listen to you," Jack responded. "You can't go on. You've had a loss. When are you going to grieve, Kathy? Are you going to grieve next February? This is your time. You take your time. Everybody has their time and this is yours."

"But I don't want people to be hauled in on a weekend to replace me. Poor Mary Beth, poor Steve, poor . . ." and I started going down the list of all the hosts who might be called in.

"Kathy, you've always been there for everyone else. You're entitled."

"Yeah, but I'm the Ironman, I never need anything."

"Yes, well, even the Ironman has a bad day, Kathy. You will not be here this weekend. I don't want to see your face."

I couldn't argue anymore, all I could do was be very grateful.

You've got to remember, it was my *ex*-husband who had died and for most people that would not entitle me to any special attention. Then again, my colleagues knew of my closeness to Jay. Jack put out a voice-mail informing everyone of Jay's death and my upcoming absence and they all responded in some way or other. Many sent flowers. It's not the custom for Jewish people to send flowers when someone dies and yet it's certainly a lovely gesture. Jewish people tend to make donations to a cause that is usually mentioned later, after the funeral. In Jay's case, years before, he'd made it known to his wife that if anything happened to him he wanted contributions to go to the Children's Hospital in Philadelphia (one of his daughters was born premature and successfully treated there) or to the American Cancer Society because he had been saved from Hodgkin's disease.

Anyway, I realized the minute I hung up with Jack that he was positively right; I could never have gone on the air that weekend. I don't know where my head was, thinking that I could. This kind of mourning was so new to me, I didn't know what it was like, though I soon learned. I learned that grief comes in waves. Saturday I was getting my nails polished and laughing about the crazy colors that were being requested for Halloween and when the manicurist started on the third nail, I burst into tears. I went out to get a bagel and while I was buttering it, the tears came. I was paying a toll on the turnpike, and suddenly I was sobbing. I was rushing here and there and when I'd bump into someone I knew and they'd ask "How are you?" I'd burst into tears. I tried to keep busy all day so I wouldn't have to be at home. I had an awful day, and the good news is, I permitted myself the awful day. As a rule, I don't allow myself to wallow in pain, but this one was coming to me. I thoroughly wallowed in my grief.

When I got home that evening there were tons of messages and I kept busy calling my friends. At the same time, Jay's family was kept busy notifying all his friends, who ranged from Hong Kong to Paris. Jay knew everyone; he was one of those charismatic characters everyone remembers. He had a special ability to touch people in a way that made him memorable.

I got through Saturday and was relatively calm. That evening I had a dinner with business acquaintances and I said nothing about Jay's death. They didn't know him and I didn't want to bring things down. So we had a good time, laughing and talking, and these people had no idea of my sorrow. Sometimes it's good therapy to be with "strangers" and to have to carry on normally.

I was so grateful that I didn't have to work and I blessed my boss for being so insightful. I talked to my mother and after Friday, a lost day for her as well as me, she too had pulled herself together and gone out. My mother and my friends were concerned about the funeral—who was going to be with me and support me. I decided that I didn't need to have anyone special. If someone wanted to be there, okay, but nobody was obligated.

On Sunday, I got dressed for the services. Jay hated black and long ago had told me that if he died I was not to wear black to his funeral. For a brief moment I thought of wearing something really wild, like a short leather skirt, in honor of the "hide" business—I knew Jay would have gotten a kick out of it. Then I thought better of it. I wore a navy blue suit and my grandmother's pearls. I also wore my grandmother's watch and ring . . . things that meant something to me.

I went over to the temple early and a few of the people standing outside were really very nice to me. They understood Jay's importance in my life and vice versa. Over and over again I was told that Jay was "proud" of me. Most were kind, but there are always exceptions. One woman had questioned the ex-wife's being there and when told that Jay and I had maintained a friendship to the end said to someone, "Oh, did she get permission from his wife to attend?" I was told about her comments and they burned me. What got to me more was that she came up to me at the funeral and paid condolences!

194

I wasn't impressed—that's too hypocritical for my taste. I have to say that for the most part, the people who never understood my leaving Jay took the same kind of hard-line attitude and avoided me. I no longer belonged. I simply don't understand what possesses some people to think that just because you sign a piece of paper everything is over, kaput, finito. I know some people hate their exes; I heard a woman at QVC say that if her ex died she'd throw a party. But though many do loathe their former spouses, not everybody hates them. There are as many people who can say he wasn't the one for me and I'm thrilled not to be his wife, but I'm damn glad I'm his friend. Frankly, the people who knew the extent of my relationship with Jay would have been shocked if I hadn't been there. I needed to pay my respects to someone I deeply respected.

The funeral was at 2:00 and I got there at 1:30 only because daylight saving time had ended. I was running an hour late and was scared to death I'd miss the ceremony. I could just hear Jay saying, "I knew you'd never get here on time." I panicked until I realized that in all the craziness I hadn't set my clocks back, and that oversight saved me. I actually wanted to arrive early and avoid making an "entrance." I went into the temple and sat four rows from the back so as not to call attention to myself. I think the ex-wife is at least entitled to a

seat and that place became filled to capacity. I
sat quietly and soon was joined by Phyllis and
her husband as well as my aunts and uncles who
had driven in from Allentown. They came not only
because of their feelings for Jay but to be there
for me.

Once everyone was seated, Jay's family came in
from the front and sat down. It broke my heart to
see his wife and his children, who were so young to
be facing this kind of tragedy. The eulogies were
beautiful and described Jay to a tee. People talked
about how he would barge into your house, eat your
food, use your bathroom (leaving the seat up, of
course), make phone calls, ask a million questions,
and then when he was good and ready to leave, he
would exit and you'd wonder if he'd been there at
all. And how Jay loved kids and how he brought
energy and passion wherever he was and how his
booming voice entered the room before he did. The
eulogies went on. . . . He loved business, he loved
life, and then they got to the love of his life, his
wife. They spoke of their relationship and it was the
strangest feeling to sit there and listen to them
describing another woman, who was indeed the
love of his life. It was sort of a reality check for
me—no matter what I said or felt, she was his wife
and the mother of his children and I no longer
counted. If a man had six wives they wouldn't go

through the litany of all of them, just the last one, she gets the coupons. And you know something, the eulogy was 100 percent true; Jay adored his wife.

I did go to the cemetery for the interment, where yet another Jewish ritual took place. People lined up one after another and shoveled a bit of earth onto the coffin. Phyllis stood next to me and whispered, "Do you want to come forward?"

"No," I answered. "I don't want to call attention to myself."

"Okay," Phyllis responded, "but I don't want to hear from you tomorrow that you wish you had."

"You know what I want to do, Phyllis, I want to smack him, I want to yell at him for dying."

Phyllis grabbed my hand and dragged me to the edge of the grave and in front of everyone I shoveled a small bit of dirt onto the coffin. My nose was running and I was sniveling, but I did it. I hoped that some of the people watching realized that even though I was just an ex-wife, Jay meant something to me. I must say that people seemed to be a little softer; some who hadn't previously approached me did come to me and I was hugged and kissed.

In the Jewish faith, the family sits shiva at the home of the deceased for a week after the funeral. It's like a wake except the body is gone and there's less drinking than there is eating. People usually bring food and everyone sits around and talks and cries and, yes, laughs. It's a time for healing. The custom really helps the bereaved although when the week is over and everyone's dispersed, reality sets in. Jay's death would have a far greater impact on his wife than on me. She suffered an immediate loss and had to figure out things like where to go with her life and what to do with the kids. She had to look at all the corners and turns.

When the interment was over, people began to disperse. Many would be going to Jay's house. A few felt sorry for me only because they knew I'd be going home to an empty house at a time when tradition says you are not to be left alone. My aunts and uncles volunteered to stay with me or, if I chose, they invited me to go back to Allentown with them. They were so dear. Phyllis looked after me, too. She wanted to know where I was going for dinner. I planned to go to my friend Andrea's and I really was okay with that. I did not feel I had the right to go back to the Levines'. The synagogue was a public place and I felt okay being there but somehow I couldn't go into the privacy of his widow's home.

When I got to my place the phone was ringing. Phyllis was calling from Jay's. Jay's wife—widow—asked for me and wanted to know where I was. She said that I shared a part of his life and was more than welcome in his home. I told Phyllis to thank her, I just couldn't go. I didn't say that I thought it would be awkward, I just made up something or other about having to get to work. I thought that it was very generous of her to invite me, but of course she had to be special, Jay loved her. I wish her well. It won't be easy. She has those lovely girls to raise and life decisions to make but I know that she'll triumph.

As for me, I'm not angry anymore. For a good long time I was, though, and I didn't get that squared away until I sought professional help. I was angry at Jay for not taking care of himself and angry at myself for not doing something, as if there were anything I could have done. An edge had crept into my life, and I didn't even know it. My friends saw it, my family saw it—my mother told me I was doing things that weren't in line with my character and she thought I should see someone. And I was told by more than one viewer that I didn't seem the same on the air. That did it. How could I argue with friends, family, and viewers? That's when I went to see someone and that someone had me look at the situation straight on. With good counseling, I worked my way through the anger and, equally important, the denial. I had to recognize that I had suffered a great loss, the loss of a dear, dear friend of over twenty years, someone with whom I shared a lot of history. The therapist helped me put my relationship with Jay into perspective. I learned from this experience that it's important to seek help when you are "drowning," whether it's in sorrow or whatever, and you're never too old to take advantage of professional guidance.

As I said, the anger is gone. It was nobody's fault that Jay died, bad things happen to good people, but I'm sad and I know I'll always be a little sad, and a little lonely, too. True friends are hard to make and even harder to replace. I'll always have joyous memories of Jay, and I know there'll never be anyone like him again, never. After God made Jay Levine, the mold was broken. Good-bye, my dearest friend, and thank you for being part of my life.

9

QVC and Me,
or,
What's a Nice Jewish Girl
Doing in a Job Like This?

Life, as they say, goes on.

Recently I celebrated the anniversary of one of my finest achievements—ten years at the same job! Yep, on November 24, 1996, QVC celebrated its tenth anniversary, and Kathy Levine celebrated her tenth year with QVC. What a kick! Who would believe that I actually held on to a job for a decade! I haven't done anything for ten years straight, except maybe kvetch.

QVC wanted to make the anniversary celebration something really special and I think we succeeded. We had a huge blowout featuring low prices and video clips of shows from the opening day. We went on the air at the same exact time that we opened QVC originally, at 7:30 P.M. on November 24, only this time it was 1996 not 1986. Bob Bowersox and I entered the set exactly as we had done on the first show—he from stage left and me from stage right. We met in the middle and turned to face our audience. Get this: I was wearing the very dress I'd worn in 1986, a Nicole Miller. (I had good taste even then.) Nicole Miller is still in business, as well she should be; she's terrific. I put that dress aside and kept it all these years as a sort of sentimental gesture. Who knew that I would be wearing it again ten years down the road? It's a plum-colored knit with dolman sleeves and a straight body line—very eighties, and, let me tell you, I was real proud to get my tookus into it in the nineties.

When I put on the dress for the anniversary show, the hem was eight inches below my knees. I looked like my bubbe. I wanted to be authentic, but not that authentic. I was afraid that someone who didn't know the history of QVC would tune in and see this old fart wearing a fashion faux pas. So, I made one simple adjustment—I belted the dress at the waist and yanked up the skirt to a more "today" length and presto, I was in style.

QVC and Me

People were amazed that I wore a ten-year-old dress. Why? I've always said that good is good. Of course there was a moth hole or two in the hem, but who cares! Bob couldn't believe I was wearing the very same outfit and laughingly said that even if he had kept the jacket he'd worn, he'd never be able to button it.

"How did you get into that dress?" he asked.

"The power of positive thinking," I replied.

That dress has real significance for me and I plan to keep it forever, not to wear but for sentimental reasons. Hey, I may even get to wear it again. Who knows how many anniversaries I'll be shlepping it out for?

In attempting to re-create accurately my television debut, I also wore a double strand of pearls as I had done in '86, only this time they weren't my grandmother's, they were from the Joan Rivers Collection because Joan's been like a mother to me—I mean big sister—oh, you know what I mean.

The show went for three hours and it seemed like three minutes. They showed clips of Bob and me at the first broadcast and it was hysterical. He looked like a baby, he was so young, and what a head of hair. As for me, oy. That hairdo!

The broadcast was a mixture of show and sell and all during it, they'd slip in shots of the past ten years on the screen, and then return to the present.

Bob and I had a ball together, then and now, only we're much, much more at ease in front of the camera today. How funny it is to see and how excruciating it is to judge your ten years' prior self. What a difference a day makes, but oy, what a difference a decade makes. Bob was adorable then and adorable now, but I honestly think I look better today. Boy, after all I've put into it, I'd better look better!!

The two of us had such a good laugh with each other, and *at* each other. I teased him and he teased me, but with ten years of camaraderie behind us (and I hope at least that much ahead of us), we could afford to laugh at each other.

We sold products and we also invited the audience to fax in questions or to write about favorite moments. Bob and I did our best to address all queries—within reason. A great many of the inquiries were about former hosts, people who had come and gone over the years. Of course, many of them wondered about Jeff. We told the audience that we hadn't heard from him in some time but that, as far as we knew, he was somewhere in the Midwest and doing okay.

Viewers also wanted to know what happened to Molly Daly, a very popular host who'd been gone for years. We told them that, according to what we'd heard, Molly had gone off to Nashville to become a country-western singer. The next day we got an e-mail from Molly. She had watched the show and got a big kick out of our alluding to her as a country-western singer. She was, in fact, doing quite unglamorous work right in Philadelphia. "I'm an account executive at a local talk-news station. I'm selling advertising, doing great, really loving it, and really pleased that you mentioned me."

Of course we would mention her, as we mentioned everyone who'd been part of our gang. We've grown together over the years, and, in those cases where we've grown apart, there's still a bond. We've welcomed new hosts and bidden fond farewells to old hosts who sometimes disappear into the vapor. We don't know exactly where they are but we're eager to hear from them. And the anniversary show enabled us to reconnect with wonderful colleagues like Molly. It would be fun sometime to have a real honest-to-goodness reunion of past and present QVC hosts. I think we'd have to limit it to hosts because otherwise we'd have to hire Madison Square Garden to accommodate everyone.

There are seven thousand employees at QVC and of that number, less than one hundred are "original" originals, those who started in the very beginning. Bob, Jane, Steve, Paul Kelley, and I are part of that group and so is the president of QVC, Doug Briggs. We are considered "founders."

We did a lot of reminiscing on November 24, 1996. The show was an interactive dream, the way you want television to be—very much "of the moment." The audience was watching a live show and sending in their comments and getting imme- diate response from us. What a wonderful walk down Memory Lane. Viewers remembered the time that Jane dropped a lamp off the table and nearly jumped into the camera. And the time I got caught up in some huge rugs and couldn't get out of them. The time a big Barbie doll that moved turned around and "attacked" host, Dan Hughes. (For every wacky thing you see, there's so much more going on behind the scenes and someday, I'm going to tell them all. I'm really not a safe person to be with anymore because I'm always collecting mate- rial. Ever since I started my "writing" career, I've warned any potential escort that if he dates me, he becomes grist for my literary mill; in other words, "Watch out, Buster, you could be Chapter 3!")

We had terrific feedback from our anniversary show. Bob and I were really turned on, in part because we were permitted to put aside the focus on sales somewhat and concentrate on simply being entertaining and having fun. That's very different from the norm. No matter how relaxed we seem, selling products is a serious business. We joke, but the emphasis is on giving the viewers what they want, not on comedy routines. (Wouldn't you know that despite the shift in emphasis, we did incredibly well in sales that evening. The products, of course, were excellent, but the looseness in our attitude and our devil-may-care spirit actually encouraged sales!)

As a founding mother of QVC and as close as I've been to the center of activity for the past decade, I still find it amazing to see how it has evolved. What changes since '86! I mean, we thought we were so slick and sophisticated then and we look back now and can't believe we operated in such an archaic fashion such a short time ago.

The lucky number device, for example, was an old lottery machine that was broken more often than not. A bar was missing in the apparatus and because the bar wasn't there to stop them, the numbered balls would come flying out of the machinery and we had to run and catch them! It was like the bubbles on Lawrence Welk's Champagne Hour. Today we're the last word in high tech and everything is computerized. Believe me, if anything goes flying (including the host), it's supposed to.

Is there a downside? Well, some little niceties in the personal end have been lost. In the old days everybody knew everyone else and most of us were on a first-name basis. Now it's such a big company, you couldn't begin to know all the employees.

On our anniversary show, we put in a call to the founder of QVC, Joe Segel, and he and Bob chatted about the early days. (For some ferkahkta reason Mr. Segel's name was misspelled in *It's Better to Laugh* and it's been bothering me ever since. Of all names *not* to get right!) We laughed about so many things concerning the beginnings of QVC. Mr. Segel brought up the two-by-four broom closet "cafeteria" that contained a couple of vending machines and compared it to our massive cafeteria of today, which feeds thousands of people daily. Remember? I told you about it in the first book. I also told you about Mr. Segel. He set the standards for QVC and everyone who came in after him followed the principles he established. That's why QVC grew in a positive and clean way. We were able to keep our heads above water even as other companies sank. Remember the television quiz show scandals when a lot of programs were brought down because of the rampant cheating? Well, in our end of the business, QVC maintained its integrity even as other companies created waves by vending junk or lying to the public, doing things like selling silver plate instead of silver.

There were twenty-seven selling companies when QVC started out, and of those only three are still broadcasting. Oh, there are fledgling local stations, too, but I'm talking nationwide cable, and in that arena, QVC has ridden the crest to the top. Ten years ago I was told that QVC would be the Saks Fifth Avenue of shopping at home. Joe Segel made that dream a reality because he stuck to his guns and was a real stickler.

"Give the people *more* than they expect," he used to say. "If you don't take care of your customer, someone else will be happy to."

We've stuck to Joe Segel's principles, and Doug Briggs, our current president, has added a few more. Doug's philosophy is "take care of *your* people first," and that means all of us who are here at QVC. Knowing that we're looked after makes it easier to look after the customer. Everybody wins.

Talking with Mr. Segel on that November 24 broadcast was very moving for me because he was the man who gave me my chance.

"You know, Mr. Segel," I told him, "when I started here ten years ago, I was a nobody, a shlep, and you gave me the opportunity to make something of myself. You changed my life."

His answer?

"Kathy, I was just there to help. *You* changed your life."

And that, I truly believe, says it all.

Afterword

So, what's ahead?

I get the feeling that the next ten years will probably go equally as fast and, hopefully, as joyously.

I can see it now: November 24, 2006, 7:30 P.M., they'll wheel me in from stage right. My teeth will be in a cup in my dressing room. I'll have two hairs on my head (beautifully coiffed, of course)—one will point north and the other south. I'll be wearing a knit plum-colored dress full of moth holes and a double strand of pearls. Bob Bowersox will come bounding onto the set. He'll be trim and youthful and he'll smile down at me, pat me on the head—between the two strands of hair—and the two of us will look back at twenty years of pure delight. By this time, there'll be other changes at QVC:

Joan will be senile, Spike will be stuffed, and the two of them will be wheeled onto the set.

Richard's thighs will have gone soft and the rhinestones will have fallen out of his T-shirt.

Afterword

Mary Beth will have eleven children, all boys—her own football team.

Mary McFadden will be married for the nineteenth time.

Susan Lucci will have lost the Emmy for the twenty-fourth consecutive year and will continue to laugh all the way to the bank.

Jane will have sold 200 million ferkahkta mops.

David Venable will have shrunk to a mere six feet two.

My boss will have arthritis in his right hand from issuing so many memos.

Afterword

And you, dear friends, will be tuned in from your living rooms doing what you do best, living and laughing and being good to yourselves.

As for me, I'll still be drooling on the set, still wondering what the hell I'm talking about, and still convinced that I've been lucky, very lucky. In fact, we should all be so lucky!

Kathy's Glossary of Yiddish Words

Altacocka	Old person
Bubbe	Grandmother
Challah	Braided bread
Chutzpah	Colossal nerve
Feh	Not so hot, icky
Ferkahkta	Mixed up
Hochim	Wise guy
Kosher	On the level
Kvetch	Complain
Maven	Authority
Mazel	Luck
Megilla	A big deal
Mensch	A good person

Glossary

Mishugena	Crazy
Mumzer	Bastard
Oy	Oy
Oy vay	Oh no!
Oy vayesmir	This can't possibly be happening to me!
Plutz	Drop
Pupik	Belly button
Putchky	Fool around
Putz	A jerk (literally a penis)
Shlep	Drag (verb), lowlife (noun)
Shnorrer	A "taker," a beggar
Shmaltz	Chicken fat
Shtick	A routine
Spiel	Explanation
Tookus (tush)	Rear end
Yarmulke	Round cap worn by religious Jewish men
Yenta	A gossip

Add the new definitions to the list from *It's Better to Laugh,* and, oy, already you're speaking Yiddish!

Acknowledgments

To my Mom, who continues to grow older with grace and style. I hope to follow in your footsteps.

To my entire family, Ron, Bruce, the in-laws, and the outlaws. The all-American dysfunctional family lives on with much love and many laughs.

To Amy Einhorn and her wonderful TV-watching mom, Ellie. You got me into this mess, and I am forever grateful.

To Gina Centrello and the staff at Pocket Books for your continuous belief in my crazy projects.

To Mitchell Ivers, my editor, who entered the game in the sixth inning and hit the winning run.

To Robin Rue, my agent, who cut through the red tape with a machete and got the job done. You go, girl.

To Anne Luttrell of QVC's Information Services Department. Whatever goofy questions I dished out, you returned with solid answers.

Acknowledgments

To Harvey Levin, M.D., of Philadelphia Weight Management. Thank you for your support and humor through "thick and thin." Your scale is still three pounds overweight.

To my cohosts and coworkers at QVC. You remain the reason I still love to come to work. The product is NOT the star, you are.

To you the viewers. There would be no book without you, and I am touched by your ongoing loyalties to me and QVC.

To Richard Simmons, who gives and gives. We should all be so lucky to have someone like him in our lives.

To Amy Sarah Appleton for your hilarious illustrations, the icing on the cake.

And to Jane Scovell, my cowriter, who had to drag me kicking and screaming through much of this work. You are my hero and I will follow you anywhere for Tuscan beans and a good laugh.

Love,
Kathy

Acknowledgments

Here's to Susan Ginsburg, Amy Einhorn, Mitchell Ivers, Michael Quinn and Shelly Welton; my children, Lucy, Bill and Amy Appleton; my grandchildren, Charlotte and Benjamin Sarraille and Isabelle Appleton. As for Kathy Levine, the truth is, like wine, she gets better with age.

—Jane Scovell

About the Authors

KATHY LEVINE, QVC's reigning number-one show host, is seen by more than 40 million people weekly. She holds a bachelor's degree in eating and kvetching and a master's degree in shopping. She considers running to a sale at Loehmann's as exercise and believes that as long as there are checks in the checkbook, there's money in the bank. She has two mottoes: "Wrinkles are for sheets," and "Settle for more."

JANE SCOVELL has coauthored books with Marilyn Horne, Elizabeth Taylor, Kitty Dukakis, Ginger Rogers, and Maureen Stapleton, as well as *It's Better to Laugh* with Kathy Levine. She is the author of a biography of Oona O'Neill Chaplin.

———

AMY SARAH APPLETON received her master's degree in English from Georgetown University and lives in Washington, D.C., with her husband, Bill Sarraille, and their children, Charlotte and Benjamin.